Pr ▐▐▐▐▐▐▐▐▐ orn

T0080702

"How I wish I had ... baby girl home from the hospital. Words that would have ... truth: 'we aren't born great mothers, we become great mothers.' Rachael walks alongside you as a trusted friend, encouraging and equipping you to be the mom God created you to be, and the mom *your* baby needs. *A Mom Is Born* provides professional and godly wisdom, personal stories, and an abundance of practical tools to help you manage and overcome the emotions that overwhelm you. Most importantly, Rachael helps you track the lies and intrusive thoughts you're believing and provides ways and words to replace those thoughts with truths that bring hope, healing, and confidence."

—WENDY BLIGHT, AUTHOR, BIBLE TEACHER, AND BIBLICAL
CONTENT SPECIALIST AT PROVERBS 31 MINISTRIES

"This is a book that every pregnant woman, partner, mental-health professional and ob-gyn needs to read. It is the book I wish was available to me when I had my children. Rachael provides a beautiful balance of real-life candor and relatability with informed neuroscience and practical skills to promote maternal emotional health. Her personable writing style and bouts of humor allow the reader to feel known and understood. This is a remarkable resource not just for mothers in their postpartum journey but an invaluable resource of wisdom and support for women in all stages of life. *A Mom Is Born* is sure to be a recommended read for many of my clients and a staple resource on my therapy shelf."

—KATE LEGGETT, LCMHC, LPC, RPT, COUNSELOR AND REGISTERED
PLAY THERAPIST AT CAROLINAS COUNSELING GROUP

"I would love to give this book to every one of my patients, because reading *A Mom Is Born* really reminded me as a practitioner how delicate the postpartum period can be. There are so many changes, physically, hormonally, and emotionally that occur, and it is assumed that most women will gracefully adapt. I am so relieved that Rachael has given the green light to medication when needed, because it really can make such a difference in their treatment. This book is the postpartum guide that can benefit so many women."

—LINDSAY SODOMA, MSN, CNM, CERTIFIED NURSE MIDWIFE

"After reading *A Mom Is Born*, the first thing I thought was, *I wish I had this earlier!* As a mom of four and survivor of PPD myself, this book is a necessity for every single new mother. Rachael's personal stories along with her professional experience and biblical references makes this book a must-read. You will laugh, you will cry, you will feel less alone, and you will feel empowered to keep going. Thank you, Rachael, for equipping us with the tools we didn't know we needed, for reminding us that we are so loved by God, and for giving us these words so we know that we are never forgotten in this motherhood journey. What a gift."

—NICOLE JACOBSMEYER, SPEAKER AND
AUTHOR OF *TAKE BACK YOUR JOY*

"*A Mom Is Born* was the handbook I desperately needed after having my first baby. With a biblical foundation, Rachael marries her professional experience as a therapist and personal struggle with postpartum depression to provide knowledge and practical tools, undergirded with truth, to sustain the weary new mom. The wisdom I've gained and strategies I've implemented from this book will be a game changer for baby #2. This is a must-read for any new or expecting mother."

—MEREDITH BOGGS, ENNEAGRAM COACH, HOST OF *THE
OTHER HALF* PODCAST, AND AUTHOR OF *THE JOURNEY HOME*

"*A Mom Is Born* is a must read for expectant and current mothers as well as everyone who loves and supports a mother in their life. Rachael uses this book to meet mothers in their pain, but she doesn't leave us there. She points us toward specific practical tools, toward supportive relationships, toward God, and even tenderly toward ourselves. She sheds light on 'taboo' topics such as trauma, anxiety, depression, medicine and PPD treatment and encourages us to connect with ourselves and those around us in honest ways, to introduce God's truth, and to experience true joy and healing in our lives. Through her vulnerable and authentic stories, readers feel seen, heard, and encouraged to believe that we are not alone, that there is hope in God, and that we can see ourselves and others through His eyes."

—SAMANTHA SULT, MA, LCMHC, LICENSED COUNSELOR AND
CO-OWNER OF KANNAPOLIS COUNSELING GROUP

"*A Mom Is Born* is a timely and very important book. With the practical wisdom given, this should be a handbook for new moms or for those caring for new moms. Rachael's vulnerability and relatable story is a breath of fresh air in contrast to the 'perfection' we often see portrayed in culture from new moms. The New Mom Wellness Plan would have been a game changer for me as a new mom! Well done on providing a loving and gentle guide, Rachael."

—LEE SUMRALL, MA, LCMHCS, LMFT,
LICENSED COUNSELOR SUPERVISOR AND
OWNER OF COMMON GROUNDS CHRISTIAN
COUNSELING, CHARLOTTE, NC

"This is a must read for every new mom! It is a beautiful manual for those who desire to not only survive the first years of motherhood but find a way to flourish. Rachael Elmore gives the reader practical tools to use as they navigate this huge transition. The depth and scope of this work is profound and life changing. Not to be read only once, but a resource like this provides valuable support throughout motherhood. I cannot wait to recommend to the client's I work with!"

—HEATHER DOOLEY, LCMHC, LICENSED COUNSELOR AND
OWNER OF RENEW CHRISTIAN COUNSELING, PLLC

"In *A Mom Is Born* Rachael joins brand new moms in the trenches and shows them how to find their groove in motherhood. Using her expertise, personal experience, and knowledge of the Bible, she encourages and equips moms to walk through postpartum with peace and confidence. The words in this book will refresh mothers experiencing postpartum depression or anxiety and give them practical, easy-to-implement tools to find freedom, hope, and joy in their journeys. If you are struggling with the postpartum experience, Rachael's book is for you!"

—LAUREN GAINES, MA, EDS, PSYCHOLOGIST,
FOUNDER OF INSPIRED MOTHERHOOD,
AND AUTHOR OF *UNSHAKABLE KIDS*

"In *A Mom Is Born* you will be met with a relatable, hopeful, and godly perspective on navigating the waters of becoming a mother. Rachael beautifully weaves together her own experiences as a mom with her expertise as a therapist. *A Mom Is Born* bravely acknowledges the range of experiences and emotions that many new moms feel and at the same time may not always feel permission to have, much less share or work through. Rachael packs in gritty truth, humor, along with practical tools to guide you and help you make a workable plan for this new season. As a mom of two, I absolutely wish I had this book in my hands before having my little ones. As a fellow therapist, *A Mom Is Born* is at the top of my list to recommend to the new mom and mother-to-be!"

—KRISTEN BRATTON, MA, LCMHC, NCC,
LICENSED THERAPIST AND OWNER OF WELLSPRING
CHRISTIAN COUNSELING, PLLC

# A MOM IS BORN

# A MOM IS BORN

*Biblical Wisdom and Practical Advice for*
*Taking Care of Yourself and Your New Baby*

## RACHAEL ELMORE,
### MA, NCC, LCMHC-S

NELSON
BOOKS

An Imprint of Thomas Nelson

Published in Nashville, Tennessee, by Nelson Books, an imprint of Thomas Nelson. Nelson Books and Thomas Nelson are registered trademarks of HarperCollins Christian Publishing, Inc.

Published in association with COMPEL, a writers community founded by Lysa TerKeurst.

Published in association with the literary agency of Brock, Inc., P.O. Box 384, Matthews, NC 28105.

Thomas Nelson titles may be purchased in bulk for educational, business, fundraising, or sales promotional use. For information, please email SpecialMarkets@ThomasNelson.com.

ISBN 978-1-4002-3399-1 (TP)
ISBN 978-1-4002-3400-4 (audiobook)
ISBN 978-1-4002-3401-1 (eBook)

**Library of Congress Control Number: 2022055164**

*Printed in the United States of America*
23 24 25 26 27 LBC 5 4 3 2 1

*For Hunt, the boy with the big heart who made me a mom.*
*Without you this book wouldn't exist.*
*Being your mom is the greatest honor of my life.*

*Praise be to the God and Father of our Lord Jesus Christ, the Father of compassion and the God of all comfort, who comforts us in all our troubles, so that we can comfort those in any trouble with the comfort we ourselves receive from God.*

2 Corinthians 1:3–4

# Contents

# Foreword

*by Nicki Koziarz*

The first words I said to my husband after bringing home our first daughter were "What are we supposed to do now?" We stared at her car seat, tiptoed while she slept, and just kept looking at each other in wonder.

It was a blissful first few days at home. Those newborn cuddles, the meals from our friends, and gifts showing up on our doorstep every day made it all so much sweeter.

But a few weeks later, I found myself in a space in my head I never knew was possible. When my daughter's crying wouldn't stop, nursing her wasn't working anymore, and my husband had gone back to work, I would often find myself lying on the couch with tears streaming down my face.

I was alone. Sad. Depressed. Absolutely exhausted. And very few people seemed to understand why I couldn't just snap back to life. I was sad and was experiencing postpartum depression in a way I didn't even know was diagnosable.

For months to come I would silently struggle with postpartum depression. But it would come out in the strangest ways, and I seriously began to wonder if I would ever be "normal" again.

What I would have given to have had Rachael's words in my life during that time.

When I first heard her book idea, I told Rachael that this was a book that needed to be placed in every diaper bag leaving the hospital. But now that I've read her words, I believe it even more.

No matter what made you pick up this book today, Rachael is the mom friend, counselor, and follower of Jesus you are so blessed to now have in your life. She's wrestled with these stories, words, and concepts because she didn't want to just write a book—she wanted to meet you in one of the potentially hardest seasons of your life. She wanted to give you practical help, inspiration, and hope, and she does this through every chapter of this book.

I especially love the practical side of planning she brings into chapter 3, where you'll build a Postpartum Wellness Plan. I kept thinking, *Every new mom needs to do this!*

I had the opportunity to coach Rachael during the initial stages of this book. The minute I saw her pop into our Zoom group for the first time, I could see there was something special about her. Rachael is full of compassion, kindness, and wisdom that has come from years of experience as a mom and counselor.

She worked so hard for you, the reader of this message. I listened to her struggle through ways to connect with moms who were single, who felt so alone and didn't have the support network she did. And as I read the words on these pages, I nodded my head: "She did it. She met them exactly where they are."

As a new mom, you'll be so busy, exhausted, and tired. But this book will be like medicine, rest, and hope for your soul. Read it as much as you can; those long nursing or bottle-feeding sessions are perfect for this. Apply what you feel is doable for today. And just keep taking things one step at a time.

You're a great mom. The words throughout this book will make you see it, and eventually you'll believe it. You're raising up a mighty generation. Trust and believe God knew exactly what he was doing when he placed that baby in your womb.

And one day you'll get to pass along this book, this wisdom, and this hope to another new mom and say, "I made it and you will too."

**—Nicki Koziarz**
Bestselling author, speaker, and writing coach with
Proverbs 31 Ministries

# Introduction

"How are you, mama?"
*Seventeen.*

Seventeen questions. The seventeenth person who texted me asked me how I was doing. Not second, third, or even tenth.

After I gave birth, my phone was flooded with text messages. I can now go back and revisit the first seventeen texts I received from loved ones, thanks to the cloud. At the time, as I lay in the recovery room following my cesarean section, I scrolled through the messages, still numb from the spinal block. While my son was being given his first bath by the nurses and Dad, I read these texts in this order:

"What's his name?"
"How much does he weigh?"
"How long is he?"
"What color are his eyes?"
"Was dad a big baby too?"
"Any complications?"
"Has he had his first bath?"

"Who do you think he looks like?"
"Has he been able to latch yet?"
"Does dad need dinner?"
"Who's the pediatrician?"
"When will you be discharged?"
"What's your hospital room number?"
"When can I come hold him?"
"Aren't you in heaven?"
"Aren't you *so* in love with him?"

In those first sixteen texts, no one asked how I was doing—or how I was feeling. Looking back, I wasn't offended in the slightest. I mean, I had just had my first baby. It's a big deal. It makes sense that my baby was the focus. The baby is what people were worried and excited about. Looking back, I only noticed question number seventeen when I later visited a friend who had just had a baby. As I visited with her, I heard people asking her similar questions in a similar order.

Before you think I'm an ungrateful and selfish friend, daughter, and wife, please know that I'm not criticizing my amazing family and friends. They took great care of me during that season. I would not be where I am today if they hadn't asked question number seventeen—a lot. They cared and still do care very much about my well-being.

Now, a decade later, I'm surprised that I wasn't surprised. I had just had *major* abdominal surgery. I had just experienced the biggest life event that had ever happened to me. On top of that, I had a bad reaction to the spinal block and anesthesia. But as the texts came through with excitement and concern about the baby, it never occurred to me to wonder, *What am I, chopped liver? Don't I matter too? Don't I get a "Good job, Rachael" or "Heck of a delivery, mama!" No "Way to give up your life, your body, your sleep, your job, your everything for this little bundle of joy"?*

But I didn't need all of that. What I did need was this: *Rachael, how are you?*

I get not being the subject of question number one, but as I look back, I wonder, *Why wasn't I number two?* The baby wasn't the only one born that day—so was I. All attention shifted to my son in an instant. And I've realized it's what happens to most new mothers. For many new mamas, this question—"How are you?"—never comes first. Always second, or third—or even seventeenth.

This order, although well meaning from my dear friends and family, revealed something to me. And it probably said something to you: in the excitement of a new baby entering the world, Mom is often forgotten.

And so I would like to ask you something and I want your honest, gritty, authentic answer: *How are you?*

Because that's what I'm all about. And that's what this book will address, head-on. Unapologetically, lovingly, *How are you?* Because I don't want you to be number seventeen. Because in these moments, not just a baby is born, *a mom is born.*

Allow me to introduce myself: My name is Rachael, and I'd like to be a part of your life in this season. In 2011, I became a mom—and it was hard. Really hard. So it shouldn't surprise me that during my nineteen-year career as a therapist, as I've worked with thousands of moms, I've learned that all new moms struggle. I'm sure you do too. I've fought the good fight to overcome the overwhelm, sadness, anxiety, and desperate days. As a licensed therapist, a follower of Jesus, and a survivor of postpartum depression, I want to offer you the help that wasn't there for me when I was deep in the trenches of first-time motherhood. I'm incredibly honored that you have picked up this book and allowed me to speak these words to you today.

Like your loved ones, I care deeply about your new baby. But this book isn't about your baby—this book is about you.

You've probably read a book or two on pregnancy and childbirth. You may have read blogs on breastfeeding, parenting, and sleep training. When you came home for the first time cradling your new baby, no one handed you an instruction manual for what was about to happen. You quickly discovered that your new life didn't look anything like the filtered new moms on Instagram. Sure, there are books on what to expect, but what do you do when things don't go as you expected?

There are plenty of books out there about birthing and raising your baby. This is a book about the birth of a mom. Being a mom is a process, and I'd like the honor of teaching you what I've helped thousands of women learn—and a few of the things I've learned myself along the way.

Alone on a deserted island, you may feel hopeless, depressed, and lost. You may even think there is something wrong with you. The very fact that you are struggling may make you feel guilt and shame. Perhaps you've experienced anxiety that makes it difficult to care for yourself or your baby. I believe this is often more than just an earthly struggle. I believe the Enemy attacks mothers in a vicious attempt to render them useless to raise up disciples of Jesus. For many, it can be the absolute darkest moment of their lives. It was for me.

Research has found that at least 15 percent of new mothers are plagued with postpartum depression (PPD) and/or postpartum anxiety.[1] Experts estimate that the vast majority of, if not all, new moms struggle with the baby blues.[2] And that's why I want to help you understand what's to blame, how to address it, and how our world may have failed you on preparing you for motherhood.

As we journey through this book we will learn to say "no, thank you" to the world's arbitrary rules of being the perfect parent. We will say "no, thank you" to comparison and perfectionism. We will refuse to give up on taking care of ourselves. God's will is for us to be good mothers. So, that's exactly what we're going to do. God has you, and you can do this, even if you don't know it yet.

There is hope. It is possible to become an emotionally healthy mom. I will show you how to take care of yourself and your new baby. The pride and shame associated with these struggles will be addressed in your heart. As we process and manage all these new emotions, we will learn to endure and embrace beautiful, messy motherhood.

To begin our journey together, I will ask you, precious mama, to do three things as you read through this book:

1. **Speak:** Let people know you are struggling. Share how you're feeling with your close friends. Let your church know. If you don't have a church, consider finding one you can trust. Call your ob-gyn or tell your baby's pediatrician. Ask. For. Help. Do not stay silent. Refuse to stay silent. Speak.

2. **Believe:** Believe that this will, in fact, work. Believe that you are a good mom. *A good mom.* Have hope, or at the very least, agree to let me have hope for you. Believe that there are good days ahead of you and that you can and will be delivered from this pain. Believe that, with God, you have what it takes to be a good mother. You *are* a good mom. Say it to yourself. Say it out loud. Write it on your mirror. Shout it from the rooftops. And then do it again.

3. **Learn:** There will be a lot to learn. We will explore your emotions, your childhood wounds, your anxiety, and your faith. We'll unpack what you thought was true about motherhood and reconstruct what God says about motherhood. We'll learn about how the Enemy is sucking you dry by feeding you lies and about how medicine works and how it might help. You will learn how to bond with your child. You will learn that sometimes success is keeping that baby alive and making it through another day. At the end of the day, they're alive and cared for. You have won. Extra credit if you prayed for your baby today.

I'm going to teach you everything I've learned in the last decade. I'm also going to share some of the darkest moments of my life—the moments that gripped me and that nearly drowned me. As we begin, pray that God will prepare you for the road ahead. I would even selfishly ask that you don't judge me for the honest story that I'm going to tell you. This is a no judgment zone, mama. But first, let's declare this over you, friend: you are the daughter of a King, and you are the mother of a prince or princess. Now take a deep breath and let's begin.

# 1

# The Tears on My Baby Are Mine

*Is This the Baby Blues or Something More?*

*Monster. I'm a monster.*
I looked down into the bright blue eyes of my newborn baby boy. His red hair caught the crisp sunlight as it filtered through my dusty bedroom window. His fingers were perfect. His everything was just as it should be.

But he wouldn't stop crying.

I'm no stranger to tears. As a bona fide professional crier and tear-catcher myself, emotions have never made me uncomfortable. Like a storm chaser, I run toward the whirlwind of emotions rather than away from them. I'm not afraid of the storm—I was born for it.

And yet these overwhelmed, exhausted, frustrated, anxious, sad, helpless, and hopeless feelings weren't at all what I was expecting. He was beautiful. I didn't deserve him. I wasn't supposed to be able to have any children, and yet I worried I was wishing him away. I worried that I was not enough for this task ahead of me. Could I be a mom?

The downward spiral continued. Around and around it went, until I was a worthless puddle of despair. In moments of sheer agony, I had unwanted thoughts of harming him, even though I never wanted to do so.

In the most painful, shameful memory of my life, I looked at my husband and asked him if I needed to be kept away from our son, the baby boy I would have given my life for. I was afraid I would cause him harm. I was afraid he could be in danger.

*In danger of me.*

The painful thoughts wouldn't stop and kept getting worse. Every thought was an assault on what I knew to be true and good in this world. Within a matter of days, I went from firmly standing in my identity as a daughter of the King to being branded with the mom's version of the scarlet letter—a *U* for *undeserving* and *unworthy.*

I sat at the foot of my bed and played with the edge of the frayed builder-beige carpet that badly needed to be replaced. I stared at the Pack 'n Play where my beautiful, wonderful baby boy was screaming.

My heart hurt, literally. The piercing sound of his scream made me nauseous. My heart felt like it was slowly being chipped away with a chisel; it was agonizing and full of darkness. I couldn't understand why he was crying; I'd tried everything to soothe him.

I had fed him. I had burped him. I had changed his diaper. I had set him in two different infant swings—both seemed to make him angrier. And I became angrier thinking we had wasted money on baby gear that didn't work. So I tried the bouncy seat. A third swaddle.

We rocked. We squatted (I remember a friend suggesting that). I checked the diaper—again.

Still, he cried. I knew motherhood would be hard—everyone says so. I expected to feel tired. I expected to be sore. But I never expected that nothing would help soothe my child. I never expected to feel this sad—this hopeless. I wondered if my baby would ever love me, because this sure didn't feel like love. I thought, *There's no way my friends have felt like this. So why am I feeling this way?* I felt worthless—like the world's worst mother. I wasn't a mother—I was a monster. And I didn't deserve this miracle of a baby.

*Why is he still crying?*

I spiraled downward as I moved beyond my unmet expectations to feelings of failure and despair.

I felt my fresh C-section staples pinch as I rocked him. The movement twinged my newly damaged nerve endings with every single rock. My pain worsened with each attempt to soothe him, as hot tears spewed out of my eyes and down my face. There was no stopping it. I'd never felt sadder. I'd never felt more despair. There was nothing to hope in. There was nothing to cling to.

I looked down at my baby—that healthy miracle baby—and was confused about why his hair was wet. There was a puddle of my tears on his head. *You're crying, but your sweet little eyes don't make tears yet.* My pain had literally transferred onto what I loved most in this world. *The tears on my baby were mine.*

This moment was full of sadness and shame. Pain and guilt. This image—my tears on my baby—was the culmination of the worst moment for me.

As I dried my tears off my sweet baby, my husband walked in with my breast pump equipment and an epic breastfeeding snack made for a champion. I saw him and I gasped out loud, out of desperation and frustration. I remember thinking, *Where have you been?* In that dark moment, I realized that he had been gone *maybe* ten minutes. No exaggeration, I would have sworn it had been hours. I knew at that moment I was not okay. I spent the next weeks reliving these moments over and over again. Looking back, I honestly don't have many other memories of those weeks.

What I do remember is my worry over feeding my baby. I was convinced I would be a breastfeeding mom. I mean, that's what good moms do, right? But after weeks of attempting to breastfeed, I couldn't get my son to latch. I spent weeks pumping so that my husband could give our son a bottle. Since every hour was spent either trying to get my son to latch or pumping to fill bottles, I got very little sleep. There is no word in the English language to describe the exhaustion that I felt.

In the middle of this dark season, I was texting a friend who had also just had a baby. She joked about feeling like a cow, with all of the milk she was producing. "I ran out of freezer space," she said. When that text came through, I was holding the Medela bottle in my left hand. I squinted my eyes to see what twenty-four hours of hard and painful work had amounted to. Pumping every hour for twenty-four hours hadn't produced a combined *ounce* of milk. The day before, the lactation consultant had told me that I had "a less than optimal breast shape" for breastfeeding. My son wouldn't latch. I didn't produce. My boobs didn't work. Well, fudge (except I definitely said the other word). What in the world was I supposed to do about that?

I couldn't feed my baby.

The very thing my body was created to do, the thing everyone says you're supposed to do, my body wouldn't do. I worried about what my crunchy breastfeeding friends would think. I worried about the higher rate of ear infections in babies that weren't breastfed. I worried what strangers would think of me. I recalled one friend telling me while I was pregnant, "I'm sorry, but bottle-feeding is just lazy and selfish." I felt sick to my stomach thinking about how I was going to tell my mom and mother-in-law that breastfeeding wasn't working. Would they think I was a horrible mom, lazy or selfish?

In the coming weeks, we would find out that my son had an allergy that was causing a lot of his pain. He wasn't a fussy baby.

He was a *hurting* baby. His little GI tract couldn't digest regular formula without pain. So he ended up on a formula that cost more than our mortgage. At the time, this drained our savings and then ran up our credit cards. Because my boobs didn't work, we had to spend thousands of dollars on formula. This was just one more notch on the belt of failure for me as a mom.

## I'M NOT OKAY.

There were several days during his first month of life that my son cried for sixteen hours without stopping. I would cry out, "God, save me. I have no idea how to help him. I feel worthless, hopeless, and like I don't deserve this wonderful baby." I truly felt "banished from [his] sight," just as Jonah did when he had been swallowed by the whale (Jonah 2:4). I was in the belly of the great fish at the bottom of the deepest sea. I felt so alone. I couldn't breathe. I was drowning. Life seemed hopeless and dim, and it felt like there was nothing to look forward to.

From inside the fish Jonah prayed to the Lord his God. He said:

> In my distress I called to the Lord,
>> and he answered me.
> From deep in the realm of the dead I called for help,
>> and you listened to my cry.
> You hurled me into the depths,
>> into the very heart of the seas,
>> and the currents swirled about me;
> all your waves and breakers
>> swept over me.
> I said, "I have been banished
>> from your sight;

yet I will look again
    toward your holy temple."
The engulfing waters threatened me,
    the deep surrounded me;
      seaweed was wrapped around my head.
To the roots of the mountains I sank down;
    the earth beneath barred me in forever.

(JONAH 2:1–6)

While I was in this belly of the beast, nothing made me want to smile—not Christmas, not s'mores, not the funniest memories of my closest friends. Most importantly, not my baby. The baby I was deeply in love with did not make me smile. I suddenly felt afraid to pick him up out of his bassinet. I knew something was very wrong. As I deliberately placed my hand on my husband's shoulder, with tears welling up in my eyes, I said, "We need to call the doctor."

The next day, I was diagnosed with postpartum depression.

## THE BELLY OF THE BEAST

As I sat in my doctor's office that fateful day, I rubbed my tongue over my teeth and realized that I couldn't recall the last time I had brushed them. Time moved so slowly. It seemed to stand still. *How could this be happening to me?* I wondered. *I'm a counselor. I'm the helper. I've never been the one who needed the help.*

Although I had fears of hurting my baby, I had no desire to actually hurt him. I had what are called *intrusive thoughts* about harm coming to my baby (more on that later). I was afraid to be alone with him. I was afraid that somehow, even though I never wanted to harm him, I would inadvertently do so. If you have suffered from any form of depression, you may know exactly what I'm talking about. It's not rational; it's chemical.

While I was disclosing everything to my doctor, a doctor with whom I have a professional relationship and share patients, I felt so much shame. *Well, there goes my career,* I thought. *Never getting another referral again.*

My doctor spent what seemed like hours talking to me and my husband about the upcoming weeks, and he prescribed a little white pill for me to take every morning. He told us that we needed to make a plan for the road ahead.

I want to pause here and say something very important: if you are having thoughts of hurting yourself or someone else, you must seek *immediate* medical treatment.

*

As an adult, I have realized that I had one of the roughest and most traumatic childhoods that I've ever heard of. (For a counselor to say that speaks volumes.) Divorced parents, abandonment, poverty, abuse, lack of adequate health care, hunger—you name it. I don't share this so that you'll feel sorry for me. I share this for a very specific reason: I want you to understand that the hopelessness and overwhelm I experienced as a new mom were more intense and dug a deeper wound in my heart than every painful moment of my past combined.

I experienced fear and feelings of inadequacy, of not being able to care for my son properly. I feared that I would somehow drop him, shake him—somehow, I could *hurt* this beautiful baby.

Until my son, Hunt, was about five months old, if he wasn't sleeping or eating, he was crying. It was so hard. I felt trapped because it felt impossible to try to take him anywhere. I felt the need to constantly apologize for his crying around other people, even strangers in Target.

"I'm sorry he's crying. I can't get him to stop."

"He's not hungry. I'm trying to get in and out as quickly as possible."

The reality is that no one was judging me. Most people could see I was at the end of my rope. I remember secretly wishing that just one stranger would stop me during one of my many public apologies for "mom failing." I wish someone would have said to me, "You don't need to say you're sorry. You are doing the best you can." I needed someone to *see* me. To really see me. To see my pain. And to tell me I'm loved, worthy, and deserving.

I deeply wish someone had said to me, just once, "Stop apologizing, mama. You are doing the best that you can. The truth is this: God is with you and he has a plan for you, even if you feel like you're in the belly of a great beast."

After Jonah was swallowed by the fish, he wrote the equivalent of a praise song. He prayed a prayer that rivals any Shakespearean sonnet or romantic comedy profession of love. *But God.* He had a plan for Jonah. He has a plan for *you.* And his plan is to prosper and not to harm.

> But you, LORD my God,
>> brought my life up from the pit.
>
> When my life was ebbing away,
>> I remembered you, LORD,
> and my prayer rose to you,
>> to your holy temple.
>
> Those who cling to worthless idols
>> turn away from God's love for them.
> But I, with shouts of grateful praise,
>> will sacrifice to you.
> What I have vowed I will make good.
>> I will say, "Salvation comes from the LORD."

> (JONAH 2:6–9)

An estimated 15–20 percent of new mothers suffer from post-partum depression and/or anxiety. I am the 15–20 percent. Other research estimates that these numbers are even higher. Unfortunately, few of these women seek treatment. As a result, we feel completely alone and are crippled by shame. We assume we don't have what it takes to be a mother. Many struggle with ugly and harmful thoughts. As they go through a harsh adjustment period they ask, "How do I care for myself and this new baby?" The Enemy uses this against mothers in a vicious attempt to render us useless to raise up disciples of Jesus. For many of us, it is the absolute darkest moment of our lives.

If you experience this as well, please know that you're normal, even if it doesn't feel that way. You may feel guilty, sad, hopeless, or ashamed. You may have moments of regret. You may be in some of the worst emotional pain of your life. It may be unbearable. I know that you need this agony to go away. Dear sister and daughter of the King, I promise you, it will get better. Have faith that God will bring you through this.

As you read this, you may be wondering how you can know if you're suffering from postpartum depression. In this next section we will examine the difference between the baby blues, postpartum depression, and postpartum anxiety. I know this may be a lot to take in, but don't panic. It's so important to understand the difference between these mental struggles in order to move forward. I know you can do this.

## WHAT IS POSTPARTUM DEPRESSION?

Postpartum depression (PPD) is a biological condition that is a result of the large-scale change in the endocrine system. While PPD is heavily impacted by spiritual and psychological components, it is not, in fact, rooted in solely psychological adjustment and fatigue.

PPD is a form of depression and anxiety suffered by a mother following childbirth. The symptoms of the disorder typically show up within the first four weeks following delivery. However, some mothers' PPD symptoms don't surface until six months post-delivery. I will use "PPD" to refer to both postpartum depression and anxiety since that is how these symptoms are classified in our medical system.

Symptoms of PPD include mood swings and preoccupation with the infant's well-being, which may range from overconcern to delusions. Some moms with PPD have more symptoms of anxiety rather than depression. The presence of severe ruminations (thinking the same sad and dark thought over and over again) or delusional thoughts about the baby is associated with a significantly increased risk of harm to the infant.[1]

No two women with PPD look exactly alike—we are sisters, not twins. Women with PPD can have anywhere from mild to severe anxiety and panic episodes. A mom's attitude toward her baby can vary widely. It can range from a lack of interest in her baby, to intrusive thoughts, to obsessions over harm coming to her baby, to fear of being alone with her baby. Since, in most cases, the symptoms typically show up in the first few months after childbirth, they get in the way of the mother taking care of herself and her baby. I've shared what it looked like for me, but I want to share another example of what PPD can look like.

SARAH'S STORY

The days leading up to the birth of Sarah's first child were filled with such excitement and anticipation. Preparations were carefully made for the arrival of her little princess, the precious daughter whom she had quite literally dreamed about. So, when her baby was finally delivered via an emergency C-section and Sarah was able to bring her home, it was disconcerting that all the joy she had felt seemed to dissipate into a fog of anxiety and despair. Born a bit premature, her baby was diagnosed with jaundice and they were sent home with instructions to keep her on her Bilibed (a light bed used to treat jaundice) as much as possible. This meant no holding, no walks, and a sleepy baby who was not very interested in nursing. Sarah was still recovering from surgery and was in pain, but even more than that, her heart hurt. She was full of fear and worry and had an overwhelming feeling of sheer inadequacy to face this new life that was now suddenly hers.

Sarah shared,

Even now, over sixteen years later, just recalling those days sends a chill down my spine, and a familiar sense of panic begins to rise in my chest. Anxiety and depression were not new to me. In fact, I had battled both for most of my life. But prior to my daughter's birth, I had been so happy and so carefree, I couldn't imagine anything but a blissful existence with my new family of three.

Unfortunately, as is the case for so many new moms, this was not to be. Within the first day or two of coming home from the hospital, my mood began to gradually change. I began a downward spiral that I did not completely come out of again for over a year. I had experienced depression before, but this was a whole new level of despair, for not only was I suffering from out-of-control hormones and a chemical imbalance, but I now had a little person who was depending on me, along with a mountain of new responsibilities. To say I was overwhelmed does not even begin to convey the magnitude of my hopelessness and fear. I could barely get out of bed, much less function in any sort of normal capacity.

Those days were like a nightmare from which I could not wake. I was exhausted but dreaded the panic attack that inevitably came upon me each time I fell asleep and woke to remember my reality. I couldn't watch TV. I couldn't eat. I couldn't relax. I couldn't leave the house or see people outside of my close family members. The idea of shopping terrified me. I was fearful of running out of things like diapers and formula and not being able to bring myself to leave the house. Every moment felt like sheer oppression. I found no joy in anything, not even in my beautiful baby who I had been so eager to meet only days before.

Sarah's story is one that I've heard many times before. The overwhelm and desperation are shared by many new moms. While no two moms are exactly alike, the truth stays the same: all new moms struggle. Whether with the baby blues, depression, or anxiety, we struggle.

While you adjust to new motherhood, it's important to talk about risk factors in experiencing depression and anxiety.

Some of the risk factors that increase the chances of having depression and anxiety post-delivery are

- complications during pregnancy and delivery,
- previous issues with depression or another mental health diagnosis,
- family history of mental illness,
- infertility problems before pregnancy,
- unsupportive spouse,
- delivering more than one baby (twins, triplets, etc.),
- living far away from the mother's family, or
- lack of social support.[2]

As you read this list, do you notice what are *not* risk factors? Take a moment and read the list again. What is *not* listed as a cause of struggling? Do you see anything missing that you're feeling? What about lack of faith? Or "lack of listening to mom podcasts"? Or "didn't read enough baby books before childbirth"? I also have never met a Christian mom who had PPD because she wasn't praying hard enough. You can't just pray this away. I have now heard thousands of postpartum stories. I've never seen selfishness as the cause. I've never seen laziness as the cause. Most of all, never—and I mean *never*—have I seen postpartum depression be in any way related to the absence of love for your baby.

And yet these nonexistent risk factors were exactly what I felt were to blame. I felt selfish. I felt like I was defective, missing some essential "mom" app that should have been updated before I delivered my son. I wondered if maybe I was just lazy. I quickly adopted the lie that I had a complete lack of faith and wasn't praying hard enough. Or that maybe God just didn't love me as much as he loved other moms. Otherwise he would fix my "defect." I wondered what was wrong with me and why he would let me struggle like this.

However, once I started to speak out and share, I discovered I wasn't alone. I found out I wasn't lazy. I wasn't depressed because I was selfish. I wasn't afraid to hold my baby because I was a crappy Christian. I had a condition that required treatment. And unlike most women who have mental struggles, I already knew the steps I needed to take to get help.

## POSTPARTUM HORMONES

From the first hours after you deliver, your body starts to change on the cellular level. In the first week following childbirth, the hormones estrogen and progesterone plummet like the stock market crash of 1929.

Aumatma Shah, fertility specialist and naturopathic doctor at the Bay Area's Holistic Fertility Center, shares, "These two steroidal hormones are key to creating dopamine and serotonin, two neurotransmitters in the brain that are important in feeling calm and happy. This is why a lot of women feel amazing when pregnant: Pregnancy offers a surge of hormones and neurotransmitters that help us feel great."[3]

At the same time, the hormone prolactin increases, which helps us—you guessed it—lactate. It gets the milk flowing. Oxytocin, a hormone that helps us feel those lovey-dovey attachment feelings, also increases markedly, which compensates for the decreased levels of dopamine and serotonin in the brain. In other words, in order to "spark joy," we need these hormones.

One might be able to see why we don't exactly feel like ourselves for a few months. Due to your body no longer needing to carry a baby, it purges all of the hormones that no longer "spark joy" in your limbic system. The problem is, these very hormones are a huge part of actually sparking joy in us as a whole person. Imagine this: A random stranger comes into your house and gets rid of your washer and dryer, Netflix streaming device, coffee maker, and all of your dry shampoo. But you can't just run out and replace them. They're all on backorder. No Amazon Prime next-day delivery, ladies. And that backorder could be weeks to months. This image might make you angry and frustrated, but keep reading. We will figure out how to spark joy, I promise.

It's a massive hormonal change that we go through, and it can last for six months. It can lead to fatigue, as if we need more of that. It affects our sex drive. It can make us feel depressed and anxious. It can contribute to and even cause many of the problems that we address in this book.

Are you starting to see why you don't feel like yourself? Maybe that's because, well, you aren't exactly yourself. The levels of neurotransmitters and hormones are all over the place. They are changing . . . *daily*. From a biological standpoint, you are not the same as you were before. But there is good news. *This is temporary.* It doesn't last. You will be you—not exactly the same, but maybe even better.

So how do you know if you have PPD or the baby blues? Quite simply, the baby blues are common in nearly all new moms. It's expected that you'll feel tired, overwhelmed, and just plain inadequate to take care of this precious ball of squishy goo. But the baby blues typically last for only two weeks. Postpartum depression and/or anxiety is when these symptoms last longer than two weeks. While extremely rare, it's important that I distinguish the difference between PPD and postpartum psychosis.

*Please hear me: if you have symptoms of postpartum psychosis, this book is not the first step for you to take on this journey. Your immediate first step should be to see your doctor.*

Take some time to look at the table on the next page. Which one sounds the most like you? This is very important. Examine the table closely. Pray that God would guide you. If your partner is in the picture, ask him. No matter what, talk to your ob-gyn and make sure that your assessment is consistent with the medical assessment.

In the majority of cases, postpartum depression typically needs treatment for at least the first twelve to twenty-four months and can persist for two years. When PPD isn't treated, it can lead to other moderate to severe mental health diagnoses.

This is an issue that is very misunderstood by our culture and even a lot of health-care providers. When I started opening up, well-meaning loved ones would say, "I've never heard of anything like that." I remember the shame and dread I felt in those moments. I had a hard time finding a therapist who knew how to help me.

But there is good news in this hard season of yours: you can and will get better. I got better. My patients have gotten better. I believe that God has given me the tools that will help you. I would like the opportunity to share what I have learned in treating these

## Baby Blues

Symptoms last a few days to two weeks.

Most new moms experience these symptoms:

Mood swings
Anxiety
Sadness
Irritability
Feeling overwhelmed

Crying
Reduced concentration
Appetite problems
Trouble sleeping

## Postpartum Depression

Symptoms typically show up from three weeks to six months post-delivery.

Postpartum depression may be mistaken for baby blues at first, but the signs and symptoms are more intense and last longer, eventually interfering with your ability to care for your baby and handle other daily tasks.

Postpartum depression symptoms may include:

Depressed mood or severe mood swings

Intrusive thoughts (thoughts of harming baby), which are involuntary

Difficulty bonding with baby
Withdrawing from family and friends
Changes in appetite
Problems sleeping
Reduced interest and pleasure in activities you used to enjoy
Intense irritability and anger
Feelings of worthlessness, shame, guilt, or inadequacy
Diminished ability to think clearly, concentrate, or make decisions
Anxiety and panic attacks
Thoughts of self-harm or harming the baby

## Postpartum Psychosis

With postpartum psychosis—a rare condition that typically develops within the first week after delivery—the signs and symptoms are much more severe.

Signs and symptoms may include:
Confusion and disorientation
Obsessive thoughts about your baby
Hallucinations and delusions

Sleep disturbances
Paranoia
Plans to harm yourself or your baby
Attempts to harm yourself or your baby
*Postpartum psychosis may lead to life-threatening thoughts or behaviors and requires immediate medical treatment and hospitalization.*

*"Postpartum Depression," Mayo Clinic.

women—to share with other moms, churches, and husbands of women who have struggled in new motherhood.

In Psalm 32:3 David said that when he kept silent, *his bones wasted away*. I know that staying silent about our struggles and our sin gives the Enemy power. When I started to speak out about my pain, I quickly realized that I was not alone. There are millions of women—just like you, dear sister—who are suffering right now, at this moment. I believe that when you boldly speak out, it will change the lives and hearts of you and your child.

The thing is, I wasn't designed to mother exactly like the moms in front of me. God's plan for me was different from the plan I had for myself. I wasn't designed to breastfeed. I wasn't designed to produce milk for my baby. I wasn't made to bond with my baby immediately. But there was no design flaw, no missing software, no defect. Everything was just as it was supposed to be: *I was designed to rely on Jesus to meet my every need.*

> Therefore I tell you, do not worry about your life, what you will eat or drink; or about your body, what you will wear. Is not life more than food, and the body more than clothes? Look at the birds of the air; they do not sow or reap or store away in barns, and yet your heavenly Father feeds them. Are you not much more valuable than they? . . .
>
> But seek first his kingdom and his righteousness, and all these things will be given to you as well. Therefore do not worry about tomorrow, for tomorrow will worry about itself. Each day has enough trouble of its own.
>
> (MATTHEW 6:25–26, 33–34)

God was going to feed my baby—and it was through formula. God was going to heal my body, and it was going to be through walks in the sun, therapy, prayers, love from friends and family, and Wellbutrin XR. God was going to teach me to be a mom through other mothers coming into my life and discipling me when I didn't even realize they were doing it. He had this. He has you. I know you might be skeptical. I know you think you can't do this. But you can. He will sustain you.

*He will feed your baby. And he will feed you.*

## 2

# Hold My Baby and Bring Me Snacks

*Building Your Postpartum Pack*

Researchers learned a lot about the importance of being rescued and the role of hope in our lives from a Harvard University study in the 1950s. Dr. Curt Richter did a groundbreaking study on rats.[1] (Ew, rats. I know. But before I lose you, keep reading.)

Wild rats are known to be incredible swimmers. They can swim for days without stopping. Dr. Richter's study had to do with domesticated rats and the role of doubt and hope in their decision-making and in their ability to survive.

First he measured the length of time that they could swim in buckets of water. In one group of rats, he didn't rescue them when they would start to struggle. (Keep in mind this was before animal rights was really a part of psychological academia.) But in the other group, he would rescue them whenever they would start to struggle.

Sadly, the first group, which he didn't rescue, had no hope of rescue and swam for only about fifteen minutes before they slowly sank to the bottom. These rats lost the ability to have hope because they hadn't experienced the hope of rescue.

The other group was treated quite differently. These rats were carefully monitored and rescued whenever they started to struggle. As a result, these rats had hope. They had hope of a large hand reaching in to deliver them from their exhaustion. They had that hope because they'd experienced it. And incredibly, the rats with hope were able to swim for over *sixty-four hours* without slowing.

The rats that never experienced the rescue lived in hopelessness. They never experienced that hand reaching down and letting them catch their breath and rest their muscles. Consequently, their lack of hope turned out to be deadly. It's probably obvious that I'm stressing the importance of asking for help. What if we're just like the rats? What if in our desperate exhaustion, all we need is a helping hand to give us the hope of rescue?

The friend who drops off dinner is that helping hand. Your mom coming to town and doing your laundry is that helping hand. Your Bible study group keeping your baby for you while you take a nap is a helping hand. In these repeated rescues, we find what we need to hold on to hope in motherhood.

Repeated rescues remind us that we're not alone. Repeated rescues back up that there's a point to fighting to live another day. Repeated rescues show us that there is light at the end of the tunnel. *Repeated rescues legitimize perseverance in motherhood.*

I hope that through this chapter, you will realize the importance of asking for help. Galatians 6:2 tells us to "carry each other's burdens, and in this way you will fulfill the law of Christ." There is a beautiful example of this in Exodus 17:

As long as Moses held up his hands, the Israelites were winning, but whenever he lowered his hands, the Amalekites were winning. When Moses' hands grew tired, they took a stone and put it under him and he sat on it. Aaron and Hur held his hands up—one on one side, one on the other—so that his hands remained steady till sunset. (vv. 11–12)

Moses found his people, and his friends helped him carry on. He won the battle once he let them help him. In the same way, you're not meant to do this alone. You need people to hold up your arms when they are tired from holding your baby.

Unfortunately, we don't always think about having a strategic team in place to help a first-time mom. But motherhood was never meant to be done alone. We weren't meant to be shushed as we shush our babies at the end of cul-de-sacs in our messy suburban homes. We are meant to do this together. Throughout this chapter I want to guide you through how to build your Postpartum Pack of friends and family members who can be on call to help you and give you hope.

\*

A few weeks after my first son was born, I got an email from my church that they were starting a new mothers ministry. I took it as a sign and hit reply as fast as I could type the words. In the weeks ahead my church helped me. A lot.

They made sure I wasn't alone for more than a few hours at a time. Two ladies came each day and spent three hours at a time with me. They taught me how to be a mom. They taught me how they are able to be emotionally healthy. They prayed with me. One mom from my church, who I had never met before, brought her guitar and played some worship songs. They brought me food. They helped me learn how to calm my baby. A friend who is not a mom brought DVDs and a pizza and we just hung out. Two trusted friends kept my baby overnight several times so that I could sleep through the night. We laughed together and they talked about their struggles with being a mom. I started to feel normal. They showed up when it was ugly, didn't make me apologize for it being ugly, and continued to love me through it.

At first it felt embarrassing. Here I was a therapist—a pretty experienced one who I'd like to think is generally respected in my field. And yet I needed a group of people to help me. I look back now and am annoyed by my embarrassment. Why was I embarrassed to ask for people to join my team? Even God looked at Adam in the book of Genesis and determined that he needed a teammate. Jesus had twelve disciples. Paul chose Timothy and Silas. Scripture is full of people needing a pack, a tribe, a team. Why did I think that I should be capable of doing it alone?

Consider the presidents, CEOs, ministry leaders, and respected members of our society. Pastors have associate pastors and staff. Ministry leaders have teams of people to help them with the heavy job at hand. Presidents have chiefs of staff and an entire cabinet to advise them, not to mention Congress. A film director has producers and assistants. In writing this book, I have a team of about a hundred people behind me editing, advising, coaching, helping with my kids, dropping off food, cleaning my house, and praying for me. I have thousands of followers on social media giving me feedback on how to best prepare this book you are reading right now.

I have one friend who is particularly incredible at nurturing her children. She's so patient, so kind, and rarely yells at them. She shows me how to do this with my own children. Another friend is so encouraging with her kids. A third has boundaries and a set of healthy expectations that deserves its own book. All the members of my Postpartum Pack have together taught me to be an emotionally healthy mom.

So the question must be asked: As we seek after one of the most important callings in this lifetime, why don't we have an official team that we ask to join in on the journey? If it will make us better moms, shouldn't we ask for help?

## WHO SHOULD BE IN YOUR POSTPARTUM PACK?

Your Postpartum Pack needs to be three to five people. Ideally, your spouse or partner would be one member of your pack. I want to note that my Postpartum Pack included two people who were completely new to my life who I met through my church. It is not necessary for a member to be a parent. One of mine was not a mother, and she was an amazing member of my pack. I found my pack in my husband, my mom, my neighbors, and a few church members. God brought them into my path. *I just had to be willing to ask them to join my pack.*

It's important that you carefully think through how to ask the right people to join you for this season. Before you ask someone to join your pack, you need to make sure they meet these three requirements:

1. **They need to be faithful.** Loyalty to you and to the journey ahead is so important. They need to be faithful to you and the Lord. They need to be faithful to the importance of the Lord in your path. I would want them to be someone who can commit to pray for you. Are they trustworthy? Do they do what they say they're going to do?
2. **They must be available.** We all have that friend who is so awesome and fun. However, they are so busy that they aren't available to take your calls. Maybe they are infamous for changing plans at the last minute. They say they will be there for you in a really important time, and they're not. Sometimes they have way too many friends and are

committed to too many other things. Maybe they are (gasp) flaky. Granted, all of us are busy. I'm not saying your pack needs to be full of people who don't have other commitments in their lives. But you need to look for people who *are willing to make you and your baby a priority amid their busy lives.*

3. **They must be merciful.** Being empathetic to what you are struggling with as a new mom is essential in this process. Empathy can be expressed through not making it all about them and not judging you for what you are feeling. They should be patient.

These three qualities are essential, and hopefully as you read through them, some people came to mind. The next step may be most difficult: you need to ask. Be intentional! Once you've thought of those who would be willing to help, there are three things you need to ask of each potential member of this Postpartum Pack. Start by taking a picture of this letter and texting it to a few trusted friends and family members. Ideally, I would like you to include your husband or partner in this message.

## *Example Letter for Your Postpartum Pack*

Hello, dear friend.

As you already know, I'm a new mom. And part of my journey to heal and thrive as a new mom is to reach out to a handful of people to help me during this difficult season. It's not easy for me to ask for help, but I need you. Would you be willing to join me?

I need three things from you:

1. **Will you commit to me?** For the next three to six months, will you make my text messages and my DMs a priority? I know you lead a busy life, but would you be willing to prioritize making a concerted effort to respond to me as soon as possible?
2. **Will you check in on me?** I need to be held accountable. I need someone to check on me and make sure I'm not isolated.
3. **Will you agree to help me?** I need someone to bring me tacos. Or snacks. I need someone to text me words of encouragement. I need you to FaceTime with me and show me new ways to help me. I will need prayer, support, and someone to hold my baby while she cries. I need you to tell me that I'm doing a good job when you see that I'm doing a good job. You have the power to help me heal.

I know that I've just asked a lot from you. I've asked for your time, effort, and even emotional energy. I know these are big asks, but would you agree to join me today?

With love,

_____

(Your Name Here)

I remember the first time I asked a client to send this letter to her Postpartum Pack. She cringed while staring at her phone like it was some sort of futuristic, unusable method of technology. She looked at me and said, "Really? Will people really be there for me?"

I said, "The right ones will."

Friends, I know I'm asking you to take a giant, scary, vulnerable step here. I know that all pride has to be put aside in order to assemble your team, your pack. But I firmly believe this is an essential step to take before we can get you to where you need to be: emotionally healthy as a new mom.

So, I challenge you to assemble your Postpartum Pack so that we can start meeting your needs as soon as possible.

## YOUR NEEDS

There's a big barrier that might be getting in the way of you thriving right now. So often, new moms don't know how to ask for help. You know that you're struggling. You know you're treading water and are nowhere close to the life raft that will bring you rescue. You may even know what the problem is that is causing your pain. But for some reason, new moms often think they should be able to do this on their own. That's a big wall to break down before breaking down this one: *You may not know what you need.* Or you're too tired to take the time to ask yourself what you need.

I'm a forgetful mom. I'm the mom in the carpool line searching in my wallet for a gift card to regift to a teacher for Teacher Appreciation Week. I'm the mom filling out the Valentine cards the morning of the preschool party. I'm the mom who forgets to respond to emails. I forget to schedule well visits with the pediatrician. I'm a hot-mess mom. I'm not naturally a mom with a plan.

The one thing in my life I never seem to forget, however, is to eat. I love food. I love to buy, cook, and eat food. My body always reminds me when I'm hungry. So it was bizarre, as a new mom, the first time I forgot to eat. I remember my husband frantically giving me crackers and an apple. My body was hungry, but the hunger mattered less than it had before. I looked at the food, annoyed because my body craved other things more than food.

I craved sleep. I craved a walk to my mailbox. I craved talking to an adult. I craved silence. I craved a day I wouldn't be chained to a breast pump. I craved making plans. I craved rolling down the window of my car and not wondering if the baby was going to wake up.

As a new mom, you might forget to eat, even though your stomach is yelling at you to do so. You may not realize that you need someone to check in on you. So, take this as your permission to ask your neighbors, friends, family, church, or others for help.

Here is a place to start: in the beginning, you should not spend an entire day isolated from another adult. *Separation leads to isolation, which leads to destruction.* I boldly assert that we were not meant to do this alone. So please don't.

You might need a safety check, and I don't mean this only for moms struggling with depression and anxiety. You need someone to come over and just hold your baby while you take a long shower. Someone needs to physically check on you. It's hard, but you need to ask for this.

As I've said before, many moms struggle to tell friends and family what they actually need. It's almost like the sleep exhaustion and mommy brain fog is too intense to tell their pack how to help them. Here are some of the most common requests I've gotten when asking what moms need most in the first few months after becoming a mother:

- Tell me I'm a good mom. Give me examples of things you're seeing me do well. Write me a text message or a Post-it telling me something you see me doing well. "I love the way you smile at your baby." "Look at you—talking to your baby."
- Check in on me. Make sure I don't spend an entire day isolated. Someone needs to physically check on me.
- Reassure me. Show me how you made it work. (Commission a postpartum team of three to five women who agree to walk closely with you for the next weeks of your life.)

- Tell me I'm not the only one. An estimated 11 to 20 percent of women in the US struggle with PPD. If you have struggled with PPD, tell me. Remove the shame from this struggle.
- Remind me to do the right things to take care of myself (therapy, medication, staying connected with people, exercise, podcasts, etc.).
- Remind me that this is temporary.
- Give me things to look forward to. Take me on a trip to my favorite consignment shop or to get ice cream. Join me for a Netflix marathon. Assemble a nacho bar in my kitchen to share with friends.
- Join me. Tell me, "I'm so sorry that you're suffering. That must be awful."
- Remind me that you love me—don't assume that I know it.
- Tell me that I need to talk about scary thoughts if I'm having them.

## MORE THAN NEEDS

While having these needs met is healing, there was a hard truth I learned in my journey. There was no help on this earth that could make me feel adequate as a mother. No amount of laundry help, DoorDash gift cards, or assistance with my crying baby made me feel like I could be a mother. But these acts of help enabled me to be in the headspace where I could work on my mothering. These things came together like a messy yet strong pillar that held up my new identity of *mom*.

I needed sleep, prayer, help, and a team of cheerleaders. I needed other mothers to tell me that I was doing a good job. And I needed them to be specific with how, why, when, and what I was doing to support this claim.

I needed other moms to say:

"Yes . . . you're holding him just right."
"You don't need to buy that!"
"It's normal that you feel this way."
"That's what worked for my baby, Rachael."
"You're doing it just right."
"You've got this, mama."

Maybe you don't think you'll need cheerleaders. But I think every team plays harder and longer with a group of people clapping for them. Looking back, I wish, in my sleep-deprived sadness, I could have put this need into words like I can today. I believe that you, and all new moms, need to check in with themselves to see if this is a need that needs to be met.

So mamas, let's ask for help from your pack and become a mom with a plan.

# 3

# A Mom with a Plan

## *Understanding Your Needs and the Postpartum Wellness Plan*

A few years ago, while on a minimalism kick, I was organizing my built-in bookshelves. I own a lot of books. Like, *a lot* of books. I thought that graduate school would be the final season of my library exploding. Maybe I'd start reading on a Kindle or an iPad? Nope. Looks like I'm a lover of hard-copy books and holding the pages in my hands.

While looking through my vast collection of books, I found a binder with my birth plan from 2011. I took a weeklong class at the hospital to develop this birth plan. Mitch and I took various birthing classes. We learned all of the birthing positions. How to breathe through the pain. How to visualize while pushing. How to "ride the wave" of contractions. Then I ended up having a C-section and didn't use most of these skills.

In this plan we talked through the pros and cons of breastfeeding. This helped me decide that I wanted to breastfeed. (Of course, you now know my boys never latched.) I knew I was okay with an epidural. I knew I didn't want to give birth at home. I knew that I wanted to give birth vaginally but would be okay if a C-section was needed.

A decade later, we laughed reading this birth plan. We laughed at how I thought that I could control what was about to happen to me. However, even though the plan changed, it did help us process through important decisions, which helped prevent stress and anxiety once the plan changed. We learned that *the plan matters, even if the plan changes.*

Even if you are not struggling with depression or anxiety, this plan assumes that struggles will arise, regardless of their severity. Making a plan will lead to peace and productivity in motherhood. These aspects build up a foundation that forms the hierarchy of needs. This plan will lead to joy, happiness, and fulfillment.

When I think of a mom with a plan, I think of Moses' mother, Jochebed. In Egypt, a royal decree was released that commanded the killing of all Hebrew baby boys. This plan of destruction was no good for Jochebed. She said, "Not today, Satan." She made a bold move to save her son. For three long months she hid her son from the authorities. I can only imagine how hard this must have been. I couldn't make it through a church service without my babies making their presence (very loudly) known. The Bible says she hid him until "she could hide him no longer" (Exodus 2:3).

During the three months she crafted a waterproof floating basket to place her son in. I wonder how she decided what kind of basket to use, or where to set her baby adrift to save his life from the soldiers. Exodus 2:4–8 says that she sent her daughter to keep an eye on him so that he would be found by Pharaoh's daughter. I wonder how she crafted this plan—or how she knew it was, in fact, a good plan. What we do know is that she *had* a plan. And this plan was based on her determination to save her son. Even though it was not an ideal plan, it was one of two options. And God honored the plan.

Where would we be if Jochebed hadn't made a plan? If she hadn't *asked for help* from her daughter? If she hadn't been bold. If she hadn't been brave. If she had done nothing.

Moses is one of the most pivotal people in our history. He saved what may have been millions of lives. He led the Israelites out of slavery in Egypt. He met with God and carried the Ten Commandments down from Mount Sinai. He led God's people to the promised land. I'm glad that his mom made a plan. You should make a plan too.

## YOUR NEEDS—AND A PLAN TO TAKE CARE OF THEM

If you've ever taken a psychology class, chances are you had at least one exam question on the work of Dr. Abraham Maslow. He was the psychologist who developed Maslow's Hierarchy of Needs, which helps us understand the science of human behavior and motivation. This theory suggests that people must meet needs on the bottom of this pyramid before they can focus on meeting the higher needs.

### Maslow's Hierarchy of Needs[1]

**Self-Actualization:** Reaching Full Potential
**Esteem:** Prestige and Accomplishments
**Social:** Love and Relationships
**Safety and Security**
**Physical Needs:** Food, Water, Rest, Warmth

In order to address any other need, one must first be fed and rested. It reminds me of some of the early missionaries who ventured to faraway nations with Bibles and crosses in their hands. It didn't take them long to find out that, while the Bibles were and are important, the people they were trying to witness to were hungry. They needed to be physically fed before they were ready to learn about Jesus.

We know that all human beings, not just moms, have five main categories of needs that must be met: physical, safety, social, esteem, and self-actualization. A mom cannot care about feeling good about herself and her performance at work if she's too tired to stand upright. A mom will likely struggle to focus on her self-care if her kitchen has just flooded. She can't support her friends well if she isn't receiving love from any source in her life. She's not going to be able to feel like a good mom until her other needs are met.

The bottom level must be met before we move up the ladder of our hierarchy of needs. This is a good model to follow when making our wellness plan.

We are meant to do this together, and so, let's work together to develop a plan.

Your wellness plan will include the following:

1. Your Postpartum Pack: a team of three to five friends and family members on call to help in case of emergency
2. Warning signs that a crisis may be developing: this can look like anxiety, isolating, feelings of hopelessness, fear of holding your baby, lack of self-care, loss of sleep or appetite, etc.
3. Internal coping strategies: this includes things you can do to take your mind off your problems without contacting another person
4. People and social settings that provide distraction
5. Steps to make your environment safe and prepped for wellness

Before I ask you to dive into your wellness plan, I'd like to share mine. This is the plan that I used when facing my second delivery and my second round of baby blues/PPD. It was and is a complete game changer. It is the plan that worked for me, and it's also the plan that has worked for my clients, time and time again.

# NEW MOM WELLNESS PLAN
*Rachael's (actual) Plan*

## MY POSTPARTUM PACK

These are the people who I can reach out to and let them know I need their help.

1. **Name:** Mitch, husband
2. **Name:** Deborah, mom
3. **Name:** Karen, mother-in-law
4. **Name:** Alexas, Bible study leader
5. **Name:** Ryan, neighbor

Professionals or organizations I can contact during a crisis:

1. **OB-GYN:** Rankin Women's Center
2. **Counselor:** Jane
3. **Pastor:** Mike

## PHYSICAL

I took my medication today. YES ☐ NO ☐

Am I getting at least one four-hour stretch of sleep at a time every twenty-four hours? YES ☐ NO ☐

*If the answer is no, my partner or a member of my Postpartum Pack needs to take over a feeding so that I can get this essential stretch of sleep.*

I texted my mom to see if she can come to town this weekend so I can get some rest. Mitch is going to take over the 2 a.m. feeding tonight and I'm putting in earplugs. I'll do the 6 a.m. feeding.

Am I eating at least three meals a day with adequate nutrition recommended by my doctor? YES ☐ NO ☐

Who is overseeing my Meal Train? Vicky

Who is bringing me groceries and meals this week?

1. Instacart
2. DoorDash/Grubhub: Chick-fil-A?
3. Alexas/Rici on Wednesday p.m.

## SAFETY

Do I have a plan where I won't be alone for more than one day at a time? YES ☐ NO ☐

Who is checking in on me this week?

1. Monday—Meeting Mitch for lunch near his office
2. Wednesday p.m.—Alexas and Rici are bringing over supper
3. Friday—Weather permitting, taking a walk at the park with Kate

When is my next appointment with my counselor? In 2 weeks

With my ob-gyn? Next Tuesday at 10:30 a.m.

These are the thoughts, feelings, and behaviors that serve as warning signs that I am not okay:

1. I don't want to see anyone or talk to anyone; I feel angry and agitated with everyone.
2. The baby hasn't been feeding well and has been extra fussy.
3. I start to think that I can't do this, I've had enough, this is too hard, God has left the building.

Concerns and worries I have about:

1. **Finances:** I'm worried about paying for my son's formula. I'm going to ask my pediatrician about getting some samples. I need to ask Mitch which bills need to be paid this month.
2. **Property:** I'm going to text a friend to get someone to mow the yard.
3. **Emotional Safety:** I'm going to tell my pack how I'm managing my triggers this week.

Boundaries that will keep me safe:

1. No drop-in visitors.
2. Set the expectation that my house will be a mess.
3. Communicate needs clearly to Mitch. Ask him to take over when he gets home from work so I can take a quick walk before dinner.

## SOCIAL

Who am I spending time with? My mom, Abby, and Vicky via FaceTime

Once a day, there should be contact with a member of my Postpartum Pack. I've asked my pack to check in on me every day this week.

What's one thing that I'm looking forward to? The family beach trip this summer

When can I go to a church service? This Sunday I'll go to the 11 a.m. service

When can I meet a family member or friend for a visit/coffee? Going on a walk with Kate

Am I spending time laughing, smiling, and enjoying bonding with my baby? I'm giving Hunt a bath tonight and going to try to enjoy rocking him.

## ESTEEM

Who is reminding me that I'm doing a good job? Alexas, Lauren, and Mitch

Who is praying for my confidence in motherhood? Bible study group

**Tracking patience progress:** It grows like a muscle in motherhood.

- I'm telling myself that the goal is being fed and feeding my baby. I'm celebrating each day that I meet this goal.
- I'm staying off social media where comparison causes me to spiral.

**Coping Skills:** Things or situations that can provide distraction when I feel hopeless, anxious, and/or overwhelmed.

1. Sitting in the sun for five minutes
2. Taking a long, hot shower
3. Calling a friend
4. Petting the dog or cat
5. Watching funny videos on TikTok

**Safe Places:** These are places I can go where I'm emotionally and physically safe and that provide distraction.

1. My neighbor's house
2. My mother-in-law's house
3. My counselor's office
4. The park after I've picked up a coffee
5. My sister-in-law's house

**Prepping my environment for peace:**

1. Don't spend a day without leaving the house.
2. Prepare my space: Each night, have my partner help me prepare our home for the night feedings and the following morning. This includes:

- replenishing wipes, diaper cream, etc.
- prepping multiple changing stations, if I have more than one level of my home
- making a grocery order list for the next day
- cleaning bottles
- washing dishes
- doing a quick five-minute tidy of the main living space of my home

3. Make sure that I have time to bond with my baby.
4. Curate a good playlist of podcasts, music, and audiobooks that bring joy and happy feelings.
5. Stay off of social media, which triggers my anxiety.
6. Take a few minutes to wash my face, brush my teeth, and put on mascara.

What's my main reason for doing this postpartum plan?

I love my baby and I want to get through this to watch him learn and grow.

Now that I've shared my postpartum plan with you, I'm going to ask you to complete your own. I know that this may seem daunting, and that's okay. If it's overwhelming, start with just the names and phone numbers of your Postpartum Pack. Or text one person who's offered to bring you a meal. Start small. I know it's a big plan, but it's an incredibly important one.

Now, let's fill out this plan one step at a time.

# NEW MOM WELLNESS PLAN

## MY POSTPARTUM PACK

These are the three to five people who I can reach out to and let them know I need their help. I will need them to regularly check in on me. One person on this list can be a spouse or partner.

1. **Name:** _____ **Phone:** _____
2. **Name:** _____ **Phone:** _____
3. **Name:** _____ **Phone:** _____
4. **Name:** _____ **Phone:** _____
5. **Name:** _____ **Phone:** _____

Professionals or organizations I can contact during a crisis:

1. **OB-GYN:** _____ **Phone:** _____
2. **Counselor:** _____ **Phone:** _____
3. **Pastor:** _____ **Phone:** _____

Review the following needs weekly and make changes as needed.

## PHYSICAL

I took my medication today. YES ☐ NO ☐

Am I getting at least one four-hour stretch of sleep at a time every twenty-four hours? YES ☐ NO ☐

*If the answer is no, my partner or a member of my Postpartum Pack needs to take over a feeding so that I can get this essential stretch of sleep.*

What is my sleep plan this week? _____

Am I eating at least three meals a day with adequate nutrition recommended by my doctor? YES ☐ NO ☐

Who is overseeing my Meal Train? _____

Who is bringing me groceries and meals this week?

   1. _____
   2. _____
   3. _____

## SAFETY

Do I have a plan where I won't be alone for more than one day at a time? YES ☐ NO ☐

Who is checking up on me this week?

   1. _____
   2. _____
   3. _____

When is my next appointment with my counselor (if applicable)? _____

With my ob-gyn? _____

These are the thoughts, feelings, and behaviors that serve as warning signs that I am not okay:

1. _____
2. _____
3. _____

Concerns and worries I have about:

1. **Finances:** _____
2. **Property:** _____
3. **Emotional Safety:** _____

Boundaries that will keep me safe:

- _____
- _____
- _____

## SOCIAL

Who am I spending time with? _____

Once a day, there is contact with a member of my Postpartum Pack. YES ☐ NO ☐

What's one thing that I'm looking forward to?

_____

When can I go to a church service? _____

When can I meet a family member or friend for a visit/coffee? _____

Am I spending time laughing, smiling, and enjoying bonding with my baby? YES ☐ NO ☐

## ESTEEM

Who is reminding me I'm doing a good job? _____

What's one small win in motherhood this week?

_____

Who is praying for my confidence in motherhood?

_____

**Tracking patience progress:** It grows like a muscle in motherhood.

- _____
- _____
- _____

**Coping Skills:** Things or situations that can provide distraction when I feel hopeless, anxious, and/or overwhelmed. Examples are taking a walk, petting the dog, sitting in the sun for at least five minutes, calling a friend, soaking in a bath, and using grounding exercises explained in chapter 7.

1. _____
2. _____
3. _____

**Safe Places:** These are places I can go where I'm emotionally and physically safe. Examples are a family member's home, church, and the park.

1. _____
2. _____
3. _____

**Prepping my environment for minimal stress and peace:**

1. _____
2. _____
3. _____

What's my main reason for doing this postpartum plan?

_____

After doing this plan for myself, and then working to improve it over the years, I finally printed it out (on actual paper) and handed it to a client.

She had already had her first baby a few years prior, and she was now pregnant with her second child. She started counseling with me once she realized she was struggling with new motherhood, and I wanted to be proactive instead of reactive with my approach, especially now that a second child was on the way.

My client took the piece of paper and we spent half of the session talking through how she was going to complete it. I made suggestions and even shared a little about my own plan. Then it was time for her to take the plan home and work on it. She was going to have to make it her own—not mine. Not her friend's. Not her husband's. *Hers.* God is the expert on what we need. It's our job to do the work to listen closely to what he is trying to teach us about ourselves.

We scheduled a meeting for three weeks post-delivery. My postpartum clients typically bring their new babies to these meetings. (I love these sessions, getting to hold their babies while giving the new mamas' tired arms a break.) So, as she rocked her new baby boy, she handed me that very valuable piece of paper. I was so eager to see how she was adjusting to new motherhood when the first round had been so very difficult.

"I look at this every day. It's on my fridge, Rachael. It helps, it really does," she shared.

Before she delivered baby number two, she filled out this plan with her close friends and husband. She talked about how her husband has a copy taped to his computer monitor to help him as well. Every time she started to feel sad, angry, anxious, hopeless, or guilty, she reviewed her plan. Even though it didn't predict or prevent every hard moment in motherhood, it got ahead of so many of them. It handled them. When she was exhausted, drained, and could barely see straight, it gave her a framework to focus on. Like an anchor holding a ship in place, it gave her something to grab on to so that she wouldn't get tossed by the waves.

She shared that she asked her Postpartum Pack to send her texts daily to remind her that she's doing a good job. She made herself a goal to say yes to anyone offering to drop off a casserole or meatball subs. She had a real and concrete plan for how she and her husband were going to handle the nighttime feeding schedule. This plan was helping her, and I knew that we were on to something.

There's a list of reasons why this plan works, but here are a few for you to consider. I want to keep it simple, because you've already done a lot of work today.

1. **Human beings handle stressful situations in a far healthier way when we process them ahead of time.** Actually, talking out loud about expected hardships yields less anxiety, anger, and emotional pain. While worrying can create extra stress, mentally preparing yourself before a hard season while creating realistic expectations is incredibly beneficial. Your body and mind are ready when a feeling of panic ensues; when you have a thought like *Oh geez, what is this stress?* your mind can say, "Remember, we talked about this already. And we already have a plan." This takes so much of the anxiety out of a moment when your brain is searching for answers.

2. **Putting things on paper actually has power.** Of course, you can fill this out on your phone, download it in a PDF, or use an app. But I challenge you to actually print it and hold it in your hand. (I know, so retro, right?) I want it to feel *real.* Because it is. Holding your plan takes the stress and anxiety *out of your brain* and lets you feel like you have some control—because you do. Once you hold the plan, you will feel more empowered and enabled to implement it.

3. **This plan reminds your brain of your needs.** Like the list of rules at a neighborhood pool, when the rules are spelled out visibly in large letters in front of you, they're hard to ignore. Sure, the sign doesn't prevent all violations, but it helps. If the sign wasn't there, how many rules would be forgotten and eventually disregarded altogether? As moms, we sometimes struggle to remember to take care of ourselves in our new lives and schedules. All too often, our focus is on our new baby and on whether or not we are going to sleep one hour or five hours that night. I want to highlight—heck, throw a parade that announces—*Mom, you have needs and you don't get to ignore them.* Because that's NOT in the plan, literally.

4. **This plan is a giant, beautiful set of boundaries.** By filling this out, you're setting boundaries with your friends, neighbors, family, partner, and most importantly, with yourself. *Because the most important boundaries are the ones that we set with ourselves.* If you don't put them on paper, they can seem less real, less solid. I don't want your plan—your boundaries—to be set in sand; I want them to be set in stone.

*

While an airplane is in between flights, there is a series of preflight checks that must be done. This process typically starts with an exterior visual inspection of the aircraft for any possible damage. Sensors, cables, and structural components are examined and tested. Then the interior of the plane is inspected. The weather radar is reviewed, warning lights, fire detectors, and safety equipment checked. Landing gear is inspected and the captains' logs of the previous flights are reviewed. The preflight checklist is not as thorough as scheduled inspections, but the focus here is on the critical parts of the plane for a safe flight.[2] The focus is on keeping the pilot and passengers safe.

The plane can't pass inspection if there's not an inspection protocol in place. Without the regulations, the pilot would just be guessing, hoping, or maybe praying that everything turns out okay. While no safety protocol is foolproof, developing one is a great start to a safe flight. Likewise, a solid wellness plan is essential to being an emotionally healthy mom.

The New Mom Wellness Plan became my physical, spiritual, and emotional checklist on the most practical level. It allowed me to make sure every part of myself "passed inspection" before I attempted flight, or motherhood. When I filled out this plan for myself, I started hitting each level of my hierarchy of needs. When your needs are met, you will be able to take better care of your baby as well as taking great care of yourself.

Friend, the plan here is to meet your needs while meeting the needs of your baby. Like I said earlier, feed yourself and feed your baby, right? Those are the goals that we start with in new motherhood. This plan will help you meet your hierarchy of needs so that you can accomplish your goals. It will help you become a happy, hopeful, well-adjusted, emotionally healthy mom.

# 4

# Dad Up

## *Parenting With or Without a Partner*

This section is for everyone, regardless of your relationship status. It's not just for husbands whose wives are struggling with mommyhood or for new moms who are married. This chapter is for all followers of Jesus who seek him in all things. We are called to care for widows and orphans,[1] and I believe this includes single moms. And since 37 percent of households don't have a father in the home,[2] you are not even close to being alone in this struggle.

This book is all about motherhood. All about the hard days in the first year of having a new baby. But I would be tone-deaf if I didn't include a chapter on fatherhood. If dad is not in the picture, I am so sorry. While I could fill up a whole book talking about the role of a father, I will attempt to keep it to a chapter and help you understand how the father of your new baby can aid you in your quest to be emotionally solid.

Most of us know that dads matter. I want to share a few reasons why we need to engage dad, if it is possible and safe to do so. I also encourage you to share these facts with your baby's father. I believe that dads matter just as much as moms when it comes to the well-being of the mom and baby, and I want you both to understand the responsibility of embracing this new role of dad.

## A CASE FOR FATHERS

The primary way we start to engage dads is by being willing to ask for help. One Sunday as I sat in church, half-listening as I tried to keep my new baby quiet for the sermon, our lead pastor started talking about the upcoming women's retreat. We had the great privilege of being part of a small church plant, and the majority of the church was made up of young families with lots of new babies. (Baby dedication services took up the whole stage and had to be broken up into several services a year.) The retreat our pastor was talking about consisted of only one night away from home. He addressed the dads in the room: "If you need help with your kids while your wives are gone, well, just be a dad."

I was surprised there wasn't a standing ovation. I appreciated how my pastor commissioned dads to step up into their God-given role. It was a moment that reminded me to continue to ask for my child's father to be a dad.

I am so thankful to have a very hands-on dad as a husband. Shortly after my C-sections, he was the first person to change both of our sons' diapers. He was the first person to give them both a bath. He was heavily involved in helping me attempt to figure out breastfeeding. God was very generous with me. Mitch *wanted* to be able to do all of the things that I could do with our babies.

The first time I left my baby with my husband, I asked him, "Will you be okay?" Little did he know that I was projecting onto him my own fears that I couldn't care for my baby. He laughed, "He's just a little baby; he can't scare me."

I'm thankful that this has been my experience with motherhood. I have had a supportive and very involved partner and helper. He would help with the nighttime feedings so that I wasn't on my own. Alongside me, he wiped noses, rocked our babies to sleep, and bathed them.

I've heard other women complain that their husband has never changed a diaper. Or they'll tell me, "You're so lucky your husband helps."

I still cringe at these words. To my knowledge, no one has praised me for raking leaves, gassing up the car, or paying the mortgage. Why is this? In general, society often expects women to do it all. Whether turning toward Scripture or not, they expect us to do that whole Proverbs 31 thing where the wife keeps her house, takes care of her family, and runs her successful business all at the same time. (She also bought land and ran a vineyard.) The Lord says that her husband looks at her and calls her blessed. Is he calling her blessed for being Superwoman? People rarely talk about the Proverbs 31 woman having a thriving business. Which brings me to my point: *Gender roles aren't necessarily equivalent to godly roles.*

## GOD THE FATHER

Just as we are all created in God's image, men are created in the image of God the Father. Our God, our Father, is gracious, merciful, gentle, faithful, and just. God comforts me when I'm crying on the floor of my shower. He wraps his everlasting arms around me in the most nurturing and loving way. God doesn't come home from work, prop up his feet, and say, "I paid the bills, didn't I? Taking care of the baby? That's women's work!" God, in his nature, is the everlasting God the Father and God the Mother. And he, in his very nature, is the most hands-on dad in all of history. If we, both mothers and fathers, are called to be like him, then dads are called to take care of their babies too.

Just as it's God's will for us to be good mothers, it's also his will for dads to be good fathers. Though I certainly wouldn't tell a new dad to "man up," I would and have told clients who are new fathers to "be a dad."

As I write this, it's still a common expectation that new mothers should somehow be able to read to their babies, hold jobs, make homemade organic baby food, and get on multiple waitlists for preschool. Not to mention she should exercise, take care of the home, manage the budget, and nurture her marriage. Maybe it's time we reduce our expectations of moms and increase our expectations of the involvement we need from dads.

However, having a hands-off approach may not be completely his fault. It saddens me that we have warped our roles as new parents to the point of harming our hearts. By dads having a hands-off approach, and by us reinforcing this ideology, is it possible that we have robbed our partners of the opportunity to be dads? In turn, have we robbed ourselves of the chance to be more emotionally healthy? Let's not do this. This is the opposite of what is good. I challenge you to *let them be dads.*

Let me explain how we're going to do this.

Just like becoming a mother, learning to be a dad is a truly extraordinary thing full of peaks and valleys. It is fun and infuriating. It is rewarding and full of heartache. One of the biggest mistakes you can make is taking your baby away from their father because you don't trust him to do the job correctly.

Perhaps you think, *If he burps the baby wrong, the baby throws up. I hate wasting expensive formula or precious breastmilk.* But if that's the worst thing that happens, it'll all be okay. I have met with hundreds of women who didn't want Dad to feed, change, bathe, or soothe their new baby. The problem with this is, *it's his baby too.*

If you find yourself critiquing your baby's father, consider your next steps carefully. How do you think your partner feels when you tell him he's not rocking your baby correctly or that he needs his Mylicon drops in his bottle before you begin the feeding? Do you think this makes him want to learn to be a dad? I have talked to fathers who feel emasculated and defeated when told they're not doing it right. They are robbed of the chance to do two of the greatest things in their life: bond with their new baby and help you be emotionally healthy. Granted, if he's about to drop your sweet new bundle of boogers, certainly let him know. But he needs to figure out this dad thing—without judgment—just like you're figuring out this whole mom thing.

My boys are close to me and their dad and reach out to us in different situations. Still, when they get scared at night, it's a toss-up about whether they'll come to my side of the bed or their dad's. When they get hurt, they want us both to console them equally. They don't just want mommy, and *that's a very good thing*.

The reason they reach for dad and mom when they are stressed, hurt, or scared is because they are healthily bonded with both of us, and that attachment was developed and strengthened as we both cared for them as infants. A man caring for his baby is the foundation for his child to come to him when he or she is much older. This lays the framework for their bond for the rest of their lives and keeps an important door open for a child to come to dad when he's tempted to cheat on a test or when a daughter is a teenager and her boyfriend hits her for the first time. When a son loses his job and is afraid he can't go on any longer. Don't you want your baby to grow up having a close and trusting bond with mom and dad? There is such value in a child having a close and trusting bond with both parents.

So ask yourself this: Do you want your husband or partner to be a dad who only pays the bills and poses with coordinated outfits for the annual family Christmas card? Or do you want him to be the warrior and father that God asks him to be? Because it starts today. Right this very moment.

# WHAT IF DAD WANTS TO
# STAY HANDS-OFF?

Ideally dad would want to contribute in every way to help raise the baby. But what does your path look like if dad doesn't want to help? What happens if he simply wants to pay the bills? Or what if he's "not a baby person" and wants to wait to bond with his child until he or she is older? Here are some practical steps you can take to deal with a partner who wants to be a babysitter and not a dad.

## IF YOU CAN, TALK ABOUT EXPECTATIONS BEFORE YOU DELIVER YOUR BABY.

Discuss how important it is to all three of you for him to be involved in the child-rearing process. What kind of dad was his dad? What kind of dad was your dad? Usually, we expect our spouses will fall into the roles we saw modeled with our own parents. My view of this was very warped. So we talked about this in counseling before we even got married. If you're late to the game, that's okay. I'm a therapist; I'm overly proactive. Regardless, this is a priority that needs to be addressed. Talk to your partner about your needs. Talk to each other about what this process is going to look like.

In our premarital counseling with our pastor, he had us do a simple but helpful assignment. I still have the crinkled yellow piece of paper with this completed list in the top drawer of my desk. Our pastor gave us a blank piece of paper and told us to write down these four things:

A good husband is _____.
A good wife is _____.
A good father is _____.
A good mother is _____.

He instructed us to get out our list every year on our anniversary to see how we were doing—to evaluate how we were measuring up to what our hopes were the day we got married. We haven't remembered to do this assignment every anniversary. However, I'm proud to say that we find that piece of crumpled-up paper on a regular basis and talk about how we are so glad that we put our expectations in writing. We talk about where we need to improve and what we need from each other. I highly encourage you to do this assignment. It's never too late to work on both your marriage and your roles as parents.

TALK ABOUT YOUR FATHERS.

What kinds of things did your dads help with? Where did your dads let you down? How did they interact with your mothers? When did you feel close to your dad? How did you know that he was there for you? If applicable, how did you know that your dad loved your mom?

Ask your spouse/partner to pray about it, but not in a manipulative way. We have to communicate this carefully. Ask him to ask God what kind of dad God wants him to be. His fears, which are so normal, should be addressed. Talk about what he needs in order to feel confident with his baby and how you might be able to help him in this quest.

ENCOURAGE HIM TO SEEK MENTORSHIP WITH OTHER DADS WHO ARE INVOLVED PARENTS.

My mom friends certainly are still teaching me today how to be a mom. Dudes can do the same. Our culture makes it hard for men to talk to other men about this. They feel like it's not socially acceptable to reach out to other men for help. So how does a guy ask another guy how to be a dad? Well, the answer is frustrating yet simple: He just has to ask. *He has to put aside his pride.*

The most important part of this section is this: You and your baby will be far more emotionally healthy with an involved father. Your baby will grow up healthier if he or she has a strong bond with both parents. Plus, your partner will have a more fulfilling and meaningful life if he has a close relationship with his baby. Keep in mind, this starts when they are babies—not when they are five and need a coach for T-ball.

So, let's do this. Let's have a hard, respect-filled, and loving conversation with our partner or coparent. Let's evaluate if we're getting in the way of him figuring out fatherhood. Fatherhood is terrifying, as is motherhood. But we serve a great and mighty God who moves mountains. He can help you and your baby's father handle this.

## ENCOURAGEMENT FOR SINGLE MOMS

This part was the hardest section of my book to write. For months, I couldn't figure out why. I grew up with a single mom. She changed every diaper, wiped every tear. She braided my hair and paid the bills. Maybe being raised by a rock star like her makes being a mother that much harder. But the real issue is this: I felt guilty that I have a helpful, stable partner, when so many women don't.

Let me start by saying I am proof that having an involved mom *and* dad is not a prerequisite to a child's success and health. Of course, I'm far from perfect. I have wrestled with "daddy issues." I probably still do. But I never sought self-esteem from men in the way that the world says a little girl without a father will. I got good grades and had great friendships growing up. I worked jobs, got into college, became a counselor, and then wrote a book or two. I am a happy friend, daughter, and mother. I made it. And so can your baby.

When I talk to my mom about single motherhood, she always says one thing: "But God." I speak often about her faith and her faithfulness. She is the mom built on solid ground. She made mistakes, but there was purpose in them and purpose through them.

> Suppose a brother or a sister is without clothes and daily food. If
> one of you says to them, "Go in peace; keep warm and well fed,"
> but does nothing about their physical needs, what good is it?
>
> (JAMES 2:15–16)

This verse brings up a really important point. We can wish a single mom well over and over again. We can send her our thoughts and prayers. However, if she's suffering, if she's hungry, if she's overwhelmed, or if she's at the end of her rope, God's Word asks, *what good is it?*

Single moms, God is very clear that his people are called to care for you. I pray that a closer examination of this verse will give you permission and will challenge you to do a very hard thing: ask for help and don't apologize for needing it. Set your pride aside because there's no room for pride when it comes to raising your baby.

*Just because you're single doesn't mean that you're meant to "mom" alone.* I say this a lot in this book. I stand by it. Your Postpartum Pack will be essential in this process. As for the church, we are not allowed to overlook you or your needs. We are commissioned by God to care for you. If your people are not taking care of you in the community, then you need to talk to them. If they are unwilling to change, find another church community.

As I've spent the last few years talking to single moms, I've learned one very sobering and humbling thing: single moms have far fewer choices to make and a lot less to choose from in this world. They don't have the choice of whether or not to go back to work. Usually, they don't have the financial resources to make such a choice. They don't have to choose to stay up at night wondering how much they should pump if their breast milk is not coming in. The only choice in their situation may be formula—no one's there to help them figure out breastfeeding. No one's there to help them get through it; they just have to make sure that their baby is fed.

Single moms don't spend much energy wondering about how much sleep they're going to get. They know they're going to get whatever sleep they can. There's no stress over who's going to wash the bottles or who's going to change the diapers. They know they are the ones who are going to change the diapers. They know they are the ones who are going to get everything done. I've learned that having more choices doesn't necessarily mean that things are better. I'm not trying to make a case that single motherhood is easier than doing it with a partner. Scripture tells us that two are better than one (Ecclesiastes 4:9). However, I'd like to add that two is easier than one as well. For single mothers, each single choice helps you survive the day ahead.

Single moms have an important truth to accept: You can't do it all. You can't work full time, go to Mommy and Me meetups, and volunteer in the church nursery. You can't. Single moms often expect themselves to be able to do all of the things a partner would help with in order to prevent "messing up their kid." The irony is, if you *do* try to do all of the things, it will likely result in more stress and less quality time with your child.

Perhaps you spend your days thinking, *I need to work now. I need to do laundry now. I need to mow the lawn now. I need to make cupcakes for my baby's preschool teacher's birthday.* But you can't. So don't.

You, as a single mom, will need to utilize more resources than ever before. You will need to ask for help for many things you feel completely capable of doing. And you will need to say no to so many things.

This time in your life should not be all about "not screwing up your kid." You probably carry a heavy amount of guilt for dad being out of the picture. You may or may not be a single mom by choice. Regardless, you probably carry an amount of guilt that's not from God.

Many women don't choose to be single moms. It is not your

fault if your child's father is not in the picture. Even if you started the demise of your relationship, that does not mean a dad cannot be a dad. You may have been the worst wife in history. You may have cheated and lied. But we divorce partners, not children. Please let go of any guilt you feel.

A client recently shared, "My baby is biting and I just know it's because his dad walked out. Now he'll never be 'normal' because he doesn't have a dad." I sat across from this client on a Tuesday morning as she shared her fears. I wasn't surprised. I mean, that's what us moms do, right? We blame ourselves for anything and everything that could possibly go wrong with our children. We blame ourselves for their struggles, their health problems. We worry it was that one glass of wine we had when we didn't know we were pregnant that gave them this _____ (insert any and every possible negative experience). We ate deli meat. Unpasteurized cheese. *You name it, we blame it.*

But now it's time to stop focusing on those mom-guilt worries and get to work being a mom.

So here's the deal, single moms: You will often have fewer choices in motherhood. However, you have *more* choices that need to be made before delivery. The more I've talked to single moms, the more I realize how much has to be done *before* delivery. Just as we've talked about earlier in this book, you will have to be a mom with a plan. Yet you will need to be a mom with a more extensive plan. No slacking off here. No putting that to-do list on pause. I talked to a few single moms and they gave me some amazing advice for other single mothers:

1. Establish a simple meal plan. The easier the better.
2. Stock up on staples throughout your pregnancy: diapers, wipes, mac and cheese, toilet paper.
3. Set up multiple diaper-changing stations in the house. That way, if one goes awry, you have another. Or, if you're too tired to walk up a set of stairs, you have supplies where you are. Also, for heaven's sake, put wipes everywhere in your home.

4. Decide on a trusted friend or family member to be your support person for the first six weeks. This can be a mom, a sister, a friend, etc. They need to be ready to drive you to the hospital, pick up nipple cream, and listen to you while you cry. After you choose this person, commission them in writing and ask them to be there for you.

5. Put your pride aside. You need help. It's not your fault. It takes a village, right? When that coworker or neighbor offers to throw you a shower, say yes. When they want to watch your baby while you run to the grocery store, let them. If they want to pick up dinner for you, don't hesitate. Yes. Yes. Yes. Practice it with me. Now is the time.

6. Stop buying baby pajamas with snaps. Zippers all the way, baby. Those are life-changing solutions to desperate days and nagging nights.

7. Ask for help—online, GoFundMe, Facebook, church. It's not begging if it's necessary. Ask for what it is that you need.

8. Take advantage of postpartum and pregnancy resource centers. These organizations have a ton of free resources and staples that you will need. That's what they're there for!

9. Avoid expensive extras for your new baby. For example: a wipes warmer. Stop. Right. There. If you get your baby's bum used to warm wipes, they will scream bloody murder the moment you put one on them that's room temperature.

10. Be okay with "good enough." It's about survival here. Pick a pediatrician close by. Use the cheaper diapers. Know that Gerber baby food is totally acceptable.

11. Wear your baby. Spend the extra cash on the really nice infant carrier. In my day it was the Ergobaby 360 that was almost $200. Worth it.

12. Keep multiple sleeping areas ready in your house. The crib in one room, the swing in another, and the Pack 'n Play in the den.

13. Let go of the clean house. If you can be okay with a messy home, please do so. It's such a short season. However, if a messy space will drive you crazy, let that be one of the things you ask for help with.

So, let's make four decisions today:

1. I'm going to ask for ongoing support from my Postpartum Pack.
2. I'm not going to apologize to my people or myself for needing support.
3. I'm going to wait expectantly as my friends become family to both my child and myself.
4. I'm going to believe that when things seem impossible, God has a plan to *make beauty out of ashes.*

The process of single motherhood may seem impossible to you today. But I want to challenge you to do one more thing: decide that what feels impossible is, with God's help, actually probable. That's when God does his best work. He will sustain you. He will bring people into your life to help you. To coparent. He will lead you in the right direction to get the help you will need. He doesn't leave us or forsake us. And one of our God's favorite things is when we watch him win our battles.

> But the LORD says,
> ". . . For I will fight those who fight you,
> and I will save your children."
>
> (ISAIAH 49:25 NLT)

Decide today that he's already won, even if you don't see the victory just yet.

# SURROGATE FATHERS

When I think about my childhood, some of my happiest memories are with the Bohannon family. A sweet Christian family with three daughters, they remain some of the most important people in my life, even though we are not blood-related. These three girls have been my surrogate sisters since the moment I was born. We have done life together. They have fed me, listened to me, protected me. They are family.

John is the dad of this precious family. He is larger than life, full of dad jokes, silly, kind, faithful, and strong. Though he isn't my earthly father, he stepped in when my dad stepped out.

I have many memories of John playing board games with our families. Teaching me about Jesus. Showing me new skills. Talking politics. Telling me which boys to avoid. Giving me rides to school. Listening to my problems, no matter how small they seemed. Telling my brother how much he cared about him. Moving me into my college dorm and apartments. Picking up heavy things that needed to be moved. Standing with family at my wedding. Telling me I was doing a good job with my baby.

He would probably not say that he stepped in to be my dad. I didn't call him "Dad." But he loved me and my family well. He taught me how a man should treat the ones he loves. He taught me about the love of Jesus and my heavenly Father.

I received several surrogate fathers and mothers in this world. I have been blessed, even in my father's absence. This all happened because of two reasons: my mom asked and he was willing. My mom isn't prideful, and for that, I'm thankful. She did not allow pride to keep me from the love of so many people who weren't "family."

So, for you, mama, pray for surrogates—God will answer this prayer. Pray that God will bring other people into your family who can step in where Dad is absent. My life was full of many parents who loved me well. I believe this can and should be your story too. Jesus said,

I will not leave you as orphans; I will come to you.

(JOHN 14:18)

Our God is not a god who makes orphans. Our God is one who adopts children and cares for them. I wonder how our God is going to bring a surrogate father into your child's life.

## SINGLE MOM WITH A COPARENT

Through my years as a counselor, I have learned that it is possible for a man to be a bad husband yet a good father. I have met men who have walked out on their wives but not walked out on their children. However, while it's a common saying that we should divorce spouses, not children, there are fathers who divorce both, such as my dad did with my mom and me.

I have worked with countless people who grew up with divorced parents and still have solid relationships with both parents. I'm a firm believer that, if at all possible, children need both mom and dad, even if they don't remain, or ever get, married. I know of many men who cheated on their wives, got divorced, and maintained a relationship with their children. They have lunch with their children, take pictures with them before the prom, teach them to drive a car, hold them when they're sick, spend summers with them, talk to them about their fears, and plan Easter egg hunts.

I wish that my dad had wanted a relationship with me. But I'm eternally grateful for good fathers in this world. The fathers who try. The fathers who show up. So, while I don't want you to hear that we should set the bar low, what I am telling you is to set the bar. And if he can't raise the bar, encourage him to define the bar. There's one important factor here: does he want to be a part of your child's life? If so, let him be a dad.

Even if your child's father isn't the most perfect dad, I believe it is God's design for children to have two parents present in their life. If there is a healthy father figure in the picture who wants a relationship with your child, please don't hinder that relationship. Your child will be the one who pays the price. This is hard, but if they are a safe coparent, let them be dads, even if they were horrible partners. By letting him be a dad, you will allow yourself to be the mom you're supposed to be.

*

I want to close with a story from my mom—the ultimate single mom. Recently, while holding back tears, I told her something I had never told her before: "Mom, I'm so sorry you had to be a single mom. It must have been so crappy and horrible," I said.

She replied,

Oh Rachael, I don't regret a moment. God was so mighty. I watched him perform miracles in my life. My friends became my family. My family became dear friends. I have felt loved in a way that many people never experience. Yes, it was hard. And yes, I hated to watch you and your brother suffer. I've loved my life. I still do. I'm thankful for all that God has done.

So, mama, no matter your situation—married, separated, single, or divorced—God has something for you, something for your baby. I know your current state of motherhood might not be what you had planned or even what you wanted. It may feel impossible today. Which means you will need to ask for support. Don't try to do this alone.

Like my mom, I firmly believe that there's a plan for you and your baby in this life. I believe that God will redeem your struggle into something meaningful. Something beautiful. I believe this because he did it for me. Now let's wait expectantly and see how he will do it for you.

## 5

# You Are Not a Bad Mom

## *Making Mistakes in Motherhood*

We women tend to be our own harshest critic. For example, I've never met a beautiful woman who really thought she was so. It saddens me to see so much beauty when it falls on the eyes of the blind. Years ago, I sat in my office with a woman who could have been working as a model making millions of dollars a year. *Painfully pretty.* Yet she wept about her husband leaving her for another woman.

"I've gained a few pounds, is that why? Is it because she's younger?" she asked.

It took me a moment to respond, because I couldn't fathom that someone so stunningly beautiful could be capable of having doubts like this. Tears ran down her high cheekbones, which were a work of art. She didn't need to contour. *She even looks pretty when she cries*, I thought. (I have one cry setting, and that's "ugly cry.") How could someone so beautiful doubt herself? Is she blind when she looks at herself in the mirror?

These statements don't surprise me any longer as a therapist. They've become far too common. The fact that a woman is beautiful doesn't make her believe it to be true. Facts don't equal feelings.

Similarly, I've never met a great mother who would say that she is so. I've known some truly incredible moms. Many have fostered me. Many have given me advice that I've included in this book. But they wouldn't say they are good mothers. When I tell them that they're good, without fail, the mom in question will list the mistakes that she's made in mothering:

- "I should have gone back to work sooner. She's too attached and has separation anxiety."
- "Daycare wasn't the best fit. He was sick all the time."
- "I spoiled her by holding her too much."
- "I let my daughter sleep with me way too long, which made her less independent."

The irony of these statements is thick for me. In reality, each of these examples is *riddled with love.* Love for their baby. The fact that we are constantly trying to make the right choices for our children proves the existence of our steadfast yet imperfect love.

This may be a mind-bender, and I know this doesn't apply to every situation, but have you ever thought that maybe, just maybe, God allows children to experience their parents' mistakes so that they can become the people he wants them to be? Could these missteps and mishaps be what grow our children right back into God's will for them?

## MY MOM'S MISTAKES

My dad left when I was young. My parents divorced when I was ten, and my father wasn't in the picture after that. All of the responsibilities fell on my mom's shoulders. Paying the bills, taking care of the kids, fixing the heat—everything was on her to do. Looking back, it doesn't surprise me now that I had horrible nightmares as a child, which continued into early adolescence. In hindsight, when I examine everything that was happening in my life, it all makes sense. I was anxious and afraid as a little girl. My world was falling apart and I had no idea how to think, much less talk, about it. And this manifested through my dreams. That's the thing about trauma: we can suppress it for only so long before it rears its ugly head.

My mom jokes that she "never slept again" after I was born. I was an awful baby. I didn't sleep through the night until I was a toddler. I now wonder if going through the divorce was like another newborn phase for my mom with regards to parenting me. Most nights, I would drag a thin futon mattress, blankets, and pillows along the floor of our ninety-year-old house, down the short hall to my mom's room. I don't think I ever had to knock. She was always awake before she heard the antique crystal knob click and squeak to open the latch of the door. She would ask what was wrong and I would quietly reply, "Mom, I had a bad dream. Can I come sleep with you?"

In those difficult years, she never once said no. Many professionals in my field may frown on this grace that she extended to me. I've heard respected early childhood experts say that this behavior keeps children from autonomy and doesn't encourage a child to respect boundaries. One counselor might say that this act fosters codependency later in a child's life. But, as a scared little nine-year-old girl, I needed my mom. If "spoiling me" was a mistake, I'm glad she made it.

For many families, this routine wouldn't work. I mean, how well did my mom sleep for that year I slept at the foot of her bed? A school-age child rooming with mom disrupts the whole family. However, I was suffering; I was scared. She saw it. And she was there for me. She was there for me by making what many would call mistakes.

As time went on, it got better. I started sleeping better. My nightmares became a not-too-distant memory, and I was soon ready to return to my room. I could finally walk by her room at night and not feel the need to drag my futon to the foot of her bed. That futon became unneeded clutter stuffed under my bed. As we found our new normal, I felt safe. Though this is a distant memory for me, I heard my mom question this method not too long ago.

"I've wondered if that wasn't the right move," my mom said. She wondered if she had made a poor choice with this one decision. My saint of a mother. Yes, in the eyes of some professionals she had made a mistake. But she had been led with her heart. And her heart demanded the need for merciful moments from a mother. They offered me safety and security. Her hugs and back scratches while I drifted off to sleep aided in my own spiritual growth with the Lord. These acts of love and grace transformed how I respond during the countless hours of my life when someone sits across from me in the counseling session, broken and hopeless. I have patience and grace in those moments, and she taught me that. Her mistaken merciful moments became God's opportunity to grow me into exactly who I was supposed to be. Romans 8:28 says, "And we know that in all things God works for the good of those who love him, who have been called according to his purpose."

God works all things—even missteps and mishaps—together for the good of those who love him. He's using what you're going through, right at this very moment, to grow you into the mom you were destined to be. Will you be bold enough to learn from your mistakes and forgive the ones that you have already made?

I truly wouldn't be the person I am today without my mom's mistakes. I count myself blessed that she made them. What mistakes are you fixated on that God is going to use for his glory?

We need to realize that *the fixation on the mistakes is the true mistake.* No mother has ever gotten motherhood 100 percent right. So why do mothers fight so hard to make sure they don't make any mistakes?

In trying to avoid making mistakes, we often think about the mistakes our mothers made. Some had mothers who made selfish mistakes. Some mothers were absent altogether. Some of them were emotionally withholding or even abusive. It is a heartbreaking reality of the sinful, fallen world in which we live. If this is true for you, I am sorry. It's not supposed to be like that. Mothers are supposed to put their own needs aside again and again for their children. We are supposed to comfort our children. We are called to temper our anger. We are called to be patient and to not cause our children harm. We are to love our children well.

## METAMORPHOSIS MOTHERHOOD

About a decade ago, in an old mobile home in a small suburb of Charlotte, North Carolina, I sat on the stained couch of a client that I was there to counsel. Clipboard in hand, I was talking to a mother of three who was very pregnant with her next baby. At the time, I was trying to get pregnant and so I tried not to take deep breaths while she smoked her third cigarette. I had some unfortunate news to share, and I cringed as I opened the paperwork. She had failed her narcotic drug test for the second time. I knew what this meant. She would not meet the criterion to continue to live in her current housing complex. My role as a social worker was to explain the next steps to make sure she and her children had resources and a plan. I had the lofty goal of helping her find somewhere safe to stay in the coming weeks.

First, please hear me. As someone who enjoyed diet soda and ate deli meat while pregnant, I know I don't have much room to judge. My children spend way too much time on their tablets. I have definitely not followed all the rules. However, what happened on this day changed my life forever.

I wondered how uprooting her children and moving them for the third time in a year would impact the family.

*Will they have a safe place to live?* I wondered. *Will they be able to stay in their current school district?*

"How are you doing . . . um, ya know, with this news?" I asked the mother.

"Huh?" she asked with a bewildered stare.

"This is hard news to deliver to you. How are you feeling?"

"I'm good," she replied.

I searched her face for concern. I did the quintessential therapist "head tilt," gesturing that I was just checking to make sure she was being genuine. No fooling this therapist. I've spent most of my life learning how to read people. She was being truthful. She had little worry or concern about what was happening in her life.

I spent years of my career doing in-home therapy and social work with mothers just like this one. I met mothers who didn't feed their children or take them to school. I worked with moms who did hard drugs when they knew they were pregnant. They let their children wear soiled clothes and didn't kiss them goodnight. What overwhelmed me is that these moms didn't worry about being bad moms. They slept great at night. They were light as a feather.

*Bad moms don't worry about being bad moms. Good moms do that.*

In all my years of being a counselor, this is one of the greatest lessons that the Lord has taught me. I know we are called to not worry. We are taught to trust in the Lord and lean not on our own understanding. But hear me when I say, the fact that you are here today, the fact that you cracked open this book, the fact that your anxiety and depression *concern you*, intrinsically mean that *you are not a bad mom.*

You might not be the mom you want to be right now—but you are certainly on the right track to get there. *We aren't born great mothers. We become great mothers.* Trust that metamorphosis motherhood is the goal in this process. A butterfly doesn't begin as a butterfly. She starts her life as something entirely different, just like you.

Biologically, humans don't go through metamorphosis. There is no stage in human biology where the human goes from some larval stage to an adult stage in a dramatic transformation.

And while I understand that this is true, I can't help but laugh. What more radical physical and emotional change does the human body go through than pregnancy and childbirth? I have often read that the endocrine system goes through no more drastic change in a person's life span than the weeks following childbirth—which is one of the many reasons you are reeling from the emotional curveballs being thrown your way right now, sweet sister.

While we don't go from some sort of larva into a butterfly in a matter of days, we most definitely go through a drastic metamorphosis as we become mothers. Everything changes. Nothing is ever quite the same. And though we might not yet be well-adjusted, fulfilled, patient, kind moms, isn't it okay that we are working on it? You are absolutely not required to come home from the hospital and have it all figured out. You're not supposed to be at the finish line right now. *The goal is progress, not perfection.*

## GREAT EXPECTATIONS

I loved my baby so much it hurt. But in those first desperate days, I did not love being a mom. I didn't love how I felt. It wasn't fun to be that exhausted. It wasn't rewarding. It wasn't anything like my Instagram posts—I had this adorable squishy baby, but the photos weren't real. Now I realize that the photos I posted were what I wished were reality. I wish I had known what the true goal was on those desperate days.

It's okay for you to admit to yourself that you are having a hard time loving being a mom. *Not loving motherhood is not the same thing as not loving your baby.*

Years ago there was a Facebook post that went viral. Perhaps you saw it. It's a PowerPoint presentation explaining the generational differences in expectations and rules about how one earns the badge of "good parent." This was the slide in the presentation that became the viral meme:

How To Be A Mom in 2017: Make sure your children's academic, emotional, psychological, mental, spiritual, physical, nutritional, and social needs are met while being careful not to overstimulate, under stimulate, improperly medicate, helicopter, or neglect them in a screen-free, processed foods–free, GMO-free, negative energy–free, plastic-free, body positive, socially conscious, egalitarian but also authoritative, nurturing but fostering of independence, gentle but not overly permissive, pesticide-free, two-story, multilingual home preferably in a cul-de-sac with a backyard and 1.5 siblings spaced at least two years apart for proper development also don't forget the coconut oil.

How To Be A Mom In Literally Every Generation Before Ours: Feed them sometimes.[1]

Take a moment to let that sink in. While hilarious, there is some cold, hard truth here. I reference this meme all the time in my practice. While I do want more for our children than full bellies, I want to point out the ridiculous expectations that are often put on new mothers. Many of the expectations are cultural. Some familial. Others may be self-inflicted. However the great expectations of motherhood are received, there is only one outcome: disappointment and disheartenment.

# IN HIS IMAGE

Most believers know that we are created in God's image, as Genesis 1:27 tells us: "God created mankind in his own image, in the image of God he created them; male and female he created them." What does this mean for us as moms? We are called to be like him, to imitate the things that are Christlike. To be like Jesus. We often think of God the Father, but we rarely think of God the Mother. Yes, God is referred to as "Father" in Scripture. We use masculine pronouns when talking about him. But as he created both *male and female* in his image, then God has the attributes of a great mother and father. God has been the ultimate father and mother to us. We look to him to know how to edit our lives and choices.

Because of this, we were made to be good mothers. It's in our design. Many mothers may choose to rebel against God's design. Of course, we have the ability to sin and make selfish choices. But ultimately, God's plan for you is to be a good mom.

> He is the radiance of the glory of God and the exact imprint of his nature, and he upholds the universe by the word of his power. After making purification for sins, he sat down at the right hand of the Majesty on high.
>
> (HEBREWS 1:3 ESV)

Just as Christ is the *radiance of the glory of God and the exact imprint of his nature,* you are designed to be the radiance of the glory of God in your life.

> As one whom his mother comforts, so I will comfort you; you shall be comforted in Jerusalem.
>
> (ISAIAH 66:13 ESV)

This verse doesn't imply *if* one is comforted by his mother. It says *as*. God's expectation is that a mother's very design is to comfort, to love. You aren't broken. You aren't defective. You are dealing with each day as it comes your way. You are making progress toward becoming the mother you are meant to be. And this process may look different for each of us.

One of the Enemy's greatest tactics to kill, steal, and destroy is for us to believe that we don't have what it takes to be a good mother. What better way to attempt to dismantle the kingdom of God? We have the incredible mission to raise up believers of Jesus. We have the ability to bring them up from a young age to be set apart from the world and to live a life that is good and righteous. Our sons and daughters will prayerfully continue that great and mighty legacy. I want to tell you that you are a good mom. Say it to yourself. Say it out loud. Write it on your mirror. Shout it from the rooftops. And then do it again.

You may say that you're not ready to say you're a good mom. If so, I have homework for you today. Text three members of your Postpartum Pack and say, "Hi friend. I have a quick favor to ask. Would you text me 2 specific ways that you've seen me be a good mother to my baby? Thank you!"

One night, many years ago, I was lying in bed crying. I'd had a headache for days. I was weeks behind on work. I had finally gotten my son to sleep after hours of trying and frustration. My wonderful husband came in to get ready for bed. I asked him a big question. In return he gave me one of the best answers I've ever been given to this question: "What makes you think I'm a good mom?"

After a short pause, he answered:

You are glad when he's happy. You are sad when he's sad. When he's sick, you try everything to help him feel better. You worry about him when he's hurt. You smile at him when he smiles. You light up when you look at his picture. You miss him when he's away from you for a long stretch. You love him.

I want to challenge your preconceived notions about your beliefs of motherhood. I want you to believe that you are a good mother, flaws and all. Maybe, just maybe, that's what it will take to have the hope you need to press on. Believing you have what it takes through the power of Christ is what will deliver you. That will foster metamorphosis within motherhood.

If you still find yourself resisting this paradigm shift, ask yourself: What do I lose by believing that I am equipped or, at the very least, equip-able? Trust me, friend, there is nothing to lose and everything to gain. You have the great charge of throwing off the Enemy's lies. You are telling him he isn't your shepherd; he is the thief. You are choosing to believe that God's Word is true and that his plan is a mighty one.

You've already won, though you may not even know it yet. If you reach the end of your exhausting, spit-up-covered day and your baby is fed, the major battle has been won. Mama, you've got this.

# 6

# A Rose Garden Filled with Thorns

## *Healing Your Childhood Wounds*

We often grieve in motherhood when we come to this moment of realization: our life no longer belongs to us. For me, I felt like a "milk machine" that was chained to a breast pump and changing table. I felt like my life wasn't mine anymore. But I was wrong. Could you be too?

The fallacy is that we assume that the deed of our identity is transferred into our child's name the day we give birth (or the day we receive a positive pregnancy test, for some). Our life no longer feels like our own. Our social security card comes with an asterisk and a lot of fine print. But this isn't true. My life does not belong to my baby. My life did and still does belong to Jesus.

When I think about what it takes to be emotionally healthy, I think about what it took for me to be a good mom. I'm still learning more every day about managing my mental health as a mother. Please believe me and take heart, friends: it's possible.

Right now you're working toward emotional health. Many new moms wouldn't read a book that focuses on their own mental health. New moms often read books on how to care for their baby. Very few moms take the time to learn about their own emotional health. Ultimately, the reason moms need to read this book is so that they can raise emotionally healthy children. But that process starts when mom is emotionally healthy.

## YOUR CHILDHOOD WOUNDS CAN WOUND YOUR CHILD

I was almost a year into writing this book when I realized that I kept coming to the same realization: I couldn't help mothers learn to move forward without being willing to look backward. In other words, we must understand our past wounds and how they impact our experience in motherhood.

The hurt and the wounds of our past can still inflict damage on our future. This can be very discouraging, especially for those who have been very wounded. We want what's in the past to stay in the past, right? I'm sorry, mama, but I've learned that to be a good mother, you need to deal with wounds that may exist deep in your heart from years ago.

So let's start with the basics. A childhood wound is an emotional hurt that occurs in the first eighteen years of life. It might be the rejection of a parent, abuse from a caregiver, feeling like your sibling was the favorite, body-shaming that happened at school, the teacher who mistreated you, the friend who betrayed you, or the boyfriend who cheated on you.

The list goes on and on. The importance of examining and dealing with the list is so that this list doesn't lead to a list for your own baby.

While I do think it's possible to make it through childhood without significant trauma, I believe that we all have childhood wounds—those hurts that never healed, that rejection that still stings. None of us are immune, which means we all have some healing to do.

With generational sin, it's common that we pass our wounds down to our children:

- We are body-shamed as a child, so we body-shame our children so that they won't be body-shamed by others.
- We are rejected by our father, so we become a helicopter parent in order to prevent our child from ever feeling rejection. In doing so, we rob our children of the chance to learn to use their own tools to solve their problems.
- We fail out of college, so we instill fear and perfectionism in our child in an attempt to prevent the hurt from their possible failures.

Resist the temptation to think that this problem is too far off for you to worry about. It's on your front door, and if it's not on the front door, it's definitely in the driveway. Your wounds will become your child's wounds if you don't heal them first.

There's fantastic news here: It doesn't have to go this way. This doesn't have to be the ending to your story. The good news is that we don't have to pass on our issues to our children. There's so much hope. Let's talk about how we attack our wounds.

## THE LOSS LIST

A wound is an emotional response to a terrible life event. Trauma is how our brains absorb, think about, and react to this wound. The trauma from these wounds lives in our bodies. Going through emotional trauma leaves a mark that can't be resolved without some effort. Oh, how I wish we could take our trauma and run it through the washing machine. But friends, this isn't the way that we were designed. We were designed to feel pain from our wounds so that we learn to not touch what wounded us again.

I remember the first time I burned my finger on a hot pan on a stove. I remember my mom saying, "Be careful, Rachael. It's hot." I either forgot or ignored my mother's wise words in that moment. I reached up, recoiled, and was left with the painful burning sensation. Even after ice and aloe, the mark on my little hand lasted for days. It took time to heal. But the evidence of the burn reminded me that I didn't want to go near the stove again. It reminded me to listen to my mom and to be careful. It reminded me to proceed with more caution to prevent more pain. Trauma is stored in our brain in a way that teaches us the same hard lesson.

Trauma tells us not to get into another romantic relationship immediately after a divorce. It teaches us to hide from the sound of yelling after living in a violent home. It teaches us to avoid the things that cause fear and inflict pain.

Now, if trauma lives in the brain, then that means we have to get it out of our brain in order to deal with it. We have to take this data and download it into something real, something tangible. When we get the trauma out of our brain, we can deal with it. We do this by making a loss list.

A loss list is a road map of major losses in your lifetime that have inflicted trauma on your life. The example on the next page can help you get started on your own loss list. First, make a list of your losses, wounds, and traumas. These may include the losses of relationships, pets, family members, jobs, and even a dream or two. Then draw a timeline and mark milestones and the years when those events occurred. Like a map, this helps us measure the depth of our losses. We are able to draw a picture that helps us understand how one loss may have impacted another. This also helps us see that we are able to overcome major struggles, which shows us that we are

## The Loss List

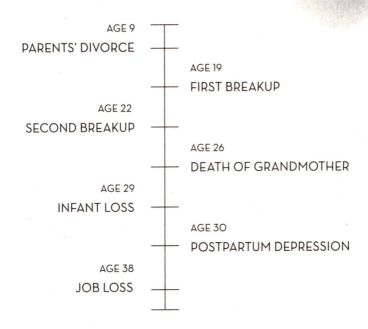

AGE 9
PARENTS' DIVORCE

AGE 19
FIRST BREAKUP

AGE 22
SECOND BREAKUP

AGE 26
DEATH OF GRANDMOTHER

AGE 29
INFANT LOSS

AGE 30
POSTPARTUM DEPRESSION

AGE 38
JOB LOSS

capable of overcoming this current struggle. Most of all, it helps us navigate through struggles to bring meaning and hope.

The idea of making a loss list may seem overwhelming. If so, then that's a pretty good indicator that you should probably be doing it. It means it's going to benefit you, no matter how hard it might seem.

I have cherished the moments that follow a client completing this heavy task. There's something about that moment when they come in after doing this assignment that's so profound, so healing. They return for a follow-up appointment with a folded piece of paper in their pocket. It may be long and daunting. However, they often say this list isn't as scary as they thought it might be. Now that it's downloaded, we can manage it; we can do something with it.

Downloading your loss list onto a piece of paper takes away the pain and power of trauma. I promise, it will free you and it will be absolutely beautiful.

While we cannot control how trauma affects us, we can control how we address the trauma. And right here, my friends, we're going to attack it and demand the healing that we deserve.

I'm going to say it one more time because I really want you to get it: *trauma doesn't just happen to you; you eventually get to happen to it.* And I can't wait for that moment of healing in your life.

After we look at our loss list, I want you to pause for just one moment. You just did some heavy lifting . . . I know it was a lot. In fact, putting together all the traumatic things that have ever happened to us in one list is a tall order. But now let's do the next essential step in your healing process. I want you to circle the three events that are the most painful when you think about your loss list. (Try not to think too hard about it—usually the first things that come to mind are the most painful events.)

Now that you've identified the most painful events on your loss list and highlighted them, I want you to write the belief about yourself that you learned from each of these losses.

For example:

1. The wound of my father abandoning my family taught me the lesson that I was unwanted.
2. The loss of a college boyfriend taught me that the girl he chose over me was better, prettier, and more valuable.
3. The loss of my baby unfortunately taught me that the world values early pregnancy less than late-term pregnancies.

Now let's go back to your loss list. Hold it in your hand and say a quick prayer. Ask God to show you what lessons you've learned and what beliefs you've adopted due to these losses. We'll address these in the next section, which deals with your corner-stone wound.

Loss #1: _____
    Taught me this belief about myself: _____
Loss #2: _____
    Taught me this belief about myself: _____
Loss #3: _____
    Taught me this belief about myself: _____

Through identifying the beliefs that came up through your loss list, is there one in particular that stands out? That's what we will be dealing with in the next section of this chapter.

PS You're doing a fantastic job. I'm proud of you.

## EXERCISE FOR DEALING WITH A CORNERSTONE WOUND

A *cornerstone wound* is a wound that is so substantial, it changes how you define yourself and affects the way you make choices. When I described childhood wounds, did one wound come into your mind at that moment? For myself, my cornerstone wound is everything that happened with my dad—the rejection, the hurt, and the abandonment. It really is my cornerstone, my defining moment. Man, oh man, have I had to deal with it extensively in order to be a solid mama.

Now I want you to look for a picture of yourself at the age this wound happened. It doesn't have to be exact, just close. You may not have this picture with you right now, and that's okay. It may require asking a family member for an old photo. While this exercise takes some time, that may be just what you need to be ready to do this exercise.

It is important to note, you may not be ready for this today. Your heart may ache. Your body may say no, and that's okay. Take your time. Be gentle with yourself. Circle this section and come back later when you've had some time to think about this assignment.

However, if you feel like you can do this, let's start healing your wounds today. Right here, right now. Hold the picture in your hand and say a prayer. Ask God to help you heal your wounds today.

Make sure you have the time to give this the attention it deserves. But also set a timer and limit the time you spend to forty-five minutes. There's a reason therapy sessions have an end—because we're not meant to stay activated in painful memories for more than this set length of time.

I want you to spend some time looking at the little girl in your photo. If you can, write down your age when this picture was taken. Close your eyes and imagine what it felt like to be her—imagine her pigtails, her dress, and the smell of the grass under her feet. Remember what she loved to do. The things that made her smile. The things that brought her joy.

Now, while looking at this picture, I want you to write a letter to yourself when you were this little girl. This is not intended to be a quick exercise—this will take some time and can be a very emotional process. It is a huge step to take in understanding, validating, and healing childhood wounds. In your letter, include the following:

1. Introduce yourself to this little girl.
2. Ask her how she's doing and write down the response.
3. Write down what you want to tell her.
4. Tell her she's going to be okay.
5. Tell her how you know she will be okay.
6. Tell her all of the things that are beautiful about her, inside and out.

7. Warn her about what you need to warn her.
8. Ask her if there's anything else she wants to tell you.
9. Tell her that her feelings are okay.
10. Tell her that you two can talk again soon.

Here's my letter to myself as a nine-year-old little girl.

Dear nine-year-old Rachael,

My name is Rachael. I'm the thirty-nine-year-old version of you. I'm writing this letter to help us both get through some hard things.

First, you're about to go through some really sad stuff. I know that you don't understand why your dad isn't home much. Soon he will leave, and it will be hard.

Your mom will cry and your brother will suffer. I know you don't understand why this is happening, but I want you to know this: none of this is your fault.

Your dad turned his life away from God years ago. He stopped praying and going to church. He stopped spending time with his friends. He is angry at God, and that's not your fault.

Much of this won't make sense until you're a grown-up. I know you're sad and confused. I know you don't know why this is happening. But I promise you: there is purpose in your pain. God loves you, even though you are hurting. God isn't okay with how your dad is treating your family. God will handle that in years to come.

Take heart, little Rachael. You will grow to be tall and beautiful. You will love Jesus and love people with all your heart. You will struggle, but your life will be full of joy as well.

It's okay that you feel rejected and angry. I wish I could warn you about the boys you will date and how they will break your heart. I wish I could prevent you from that pain, but I can't.

I want you to hear this: your dad failed, not you. There's nothing you could have done to make him stay. There's nothing you could have done to make him want to be a dad. You are a wonderful little girl. You are worthy of love. You are valuable.

We can talk soon. I believe that these talks will heal us both.

With love,

Thirty-nine-year-old Rachael

I believe that if I'm going to ask you to do such a hard assignment, I need to do it as well. I need to put in the hard work. I need to do the healing myself. I remember holding the old picture in my hands and the feeling of that photo paper with the turned-up edges. My favorite part of this letter is one simple line: *none of this is your fault.* Something happened at that moment for me. A part of the pain was lifted. A hard chapter closed firmly in my heart. I felt peace; I felt resolve. I didn't know that I needed to hear myself say it. I mean, I've been through lots of therapy; I've heard a counselor say this to me. My sweet mom has said these words to me. But for some reason, I needed to say it to myself. When I heard myself say it, I knew that God was saying it too.

So, mama, please don't skip this section and ignore it. There's so much healing in writing this simple letter. What cornerstone wound is God wanting to heal in you today? Please, friend, let God heal you as he gives you the strength to heal yourself.

# 7

# The Four Horsemen of
# the Momocalypse

## *Managing the Common Emotions*
## *New Moms Experience*

Y ou may have walked into motherhood feeling solid, feeling
secure. You might not be an emotional person. Or, like me,
maybe you feel things very deeply. Regardless of where you fall with
your personality or Enneagram type, your emotions have changed
and will change throughout your new life as a mother.

Hormonal changes and emotional evolution are both to blame
for the many emotions you're feeling right now. Motherhood is a
completely new part of your life. It's major—and I pray you don't
ignore the changes that you are currently going through.

I talked a lot in chapter 1 about the baby blues and the overwhelming sadness that can hit moms at any point during the first
year. Now that you're farther along in the book, I want to remind
you of some of the symptoms of depression to look out for:

- Depressed mood or severe mood swings
- Intrusive thoughts (thoughts of harming yourself or baby), which are involuntary
- Difficulty bonding with your baby
- Withdrawing from family and friends
- Changes in appetite
- Problems sleeping
- Reduced interest and pleasure in activities you used to enjoy
- Feelings of worthlessness, shame, guilt, or inadequacy

With the baby blues and with postpartum depression and anxiety, there are four common emotions that almost all new moms will experience in the first year: shame, guilt, anger, and anxiety. You'll see that the anxiety section is where we will do the heaviest lifting here. By far, new mom anxiety is the number one complaint I hear as a therapist. We need to address certain emotions in order to combat our anxiety, sadness, and disappointments as we journey to the other side of this dark and lonely tunnel. We will spend this chapter identifying and talking about how to manage these new emotions.

## SHAME-FILLED MOM

There is no doubt that depression and/or anxiety is to blame for a lot of the pain you are experiencing. As I dug deeper into the pain I felt as a new mom—and the pain so many women have felt—I couldn't help but ask: Are baby blues the problem or is it the *shame* of the baby blues? When I consider why it was so painful, I realize the shame worsened it. It's like the soldier who endures a stab wound yet dies from infection. I believe shame is what causes the wounds of the baby blues to fester, infect, and destroy. The crying was painful. But my tears on my baby were shameful. I was embarrassed for people to know. I was fearful of the looks I would and did receive—the "I can't believe she just admitted to that" looks. Yup, those looks. I got them. And I am asking you, my reader, to learn to be okay with them.

With any mental struggle, you may have a deep and painful wound. If you choose to not treat it, it will likely get worse. If you keep it covered with shame, it will fester. Then it will be much more painful and might take more treatment to heal.

What if you weren't ashamed of your struggle? What if you wore it like a badge of honor? Does it sound crazy? Because that's what I decided to do. *Once I refused to stay ashamed, my emotions caused me less pain.*

A few years ago, when I started writing this book, a new fear began to take root. I thought, *What will my son think when he is old enough to read this book? What will he think of me, his mommy?* This fear brought up feelings of shame.

My older son is a follower of Jesus. He knows that I had a hard time learning to be a mom and that was absolutely no fault of his own. He knows that I love him and his brother more than any person or thing on this planet. He knows that I had thoughts that the Enemy had a field day with. However, he knows (and will be frequently reminded) that God is using my pain for his glory. Period.

So I refused to stay silent. I remember the first conversation I had with my older son about this book. I was worried he would be embarrassed or ashamed of his struggling mom.

He said, "But, Mom, will this help other moms feel better? Because that's what makes God happy. And that's what makes me happy."

To my surprise, my little boy helped me find freedom in my shame. He made the shame small by reminding me that our God is oh so very big.

Like this moment in my life, I challenge you to pray about one trusted friend or family member you can tell how you're feeling.

This needs to be a loyal member of your pack. Someone fiercely strong and who loves the Lord. Text her right now. Tell her that you might have some depression. That you are struggling with the baby blues. Scary, I know. After she responds (supportive and loving, I would hope), write down how you feel. Pray. Make a vow to not be ashamed of your struggle. Then, watch God start to set you free from shame.

## GUILT-STRICKEN MOM

Shame is different from guilt. Guilt is often from God. It has purpose. Through the Holy Spirit God has given us, we experience the feelings of guilt when we have done something wrong. We feel guilt when we yell at our kids. We feel guilt when we lie to a friend. We feel guilt when we make excuses for something we should have taken ownership of.

When we feel guilt in these situations, it's to motivate us to change. It is meant to lead us to confess the lie. It's to help us stop telling the lies. It's so that we examine and change our parenting. Guilt is God's prompt to rebuild, to reassess, to redirect.

\*

I love when the hashtag #nobodyshame started to trend years ago. I have struggled with my weight almost my entire life. No matter what I do, I will always be a healthy, curvy woman. The older I get, the more I love the body that I'm in. While it is very important that we take good care of our bodies, we shouldn't be ashamed of them.

When #nobodyshame took off, trolls on social media were no longer allowed to body-shame celebrities for gaining weight without internet backlash. I love the change that this has brought to our world, even if it is a part of "cancel" culture. I wonder, why didn't

#nobodyguilt take off? That's not a trending hashtag on socials. #Bodypositivity has over 7.3 million shares today on Instagram. People don't feel guilt over the state of their bodies. They may feel guilt over some decisions that have contributed to the state of their bodies. (Me years ago with way too many brownies.) Body shame is the source of the destruction. And it's what typically eggs us on to give up and give in by eating brownie number four. To tell the lie again. To not repent for taking our anger out on our children.

*Guilt is of God. Shame is of Satan.*

One easy way to remember this is by using the *G* and *S* combinations. Guilt is a tool that can be used for a mighty purpose. Shame is a tool that is often used by the Enemy to launch our lives into failure and demise.

Now, not all guilt is of God, and not all shame is of Satan. I am saying that they are different mental and spiritual states, and they serve very different purposes.

What purpose does shame serve? According to Merriam-Webster, *shame* is defined as "a painful emotion caused by consciousness of guilt, shortcoming, or impropriety."[1] It's also "a condition of humiliating disgrace or disrepute." While shame can result from the presence of sin, it is often the state of pain because of what we perceive as our inadequacy, failures, or defectiveness.

A couple of years ago, one of my boys got in trouble at school. He did something that embarrassed me as a mom. It wounded my pride. Therefore, when talking to him about what happened, I lost it. I yelled at a level that wasn't appropriate. I said something to him that was hurtful. It was over the line—I was wounding him because of my pride.

Right before I was about to say something really wounding, I felt a pain deep in my stomach, deep in my soul. I knew I was about to do real damage. I said, "Buddy, Mommy needs to take a walk. We'll talk about this later." Dad had just come home from work. I took that messy-crying walk around the block.

The feeling that crept in when I felt the pain in my stomach was guilt. As I took that long walk, I prayed about what had happened. I texted my Bible study group and asked them to pray for me. I repented to the Lord, and I returned home and apologized to my son. I explained to him that I went too far and asked him for forgiveness. We worked it out. During that experience, it was guilt I felt, not shame. That's because shame steals and guilt gives.

The guilt served a purpose. The next time I felt myself wanting to take out my frustration on my children, I remembered the guilt from the long walk I took that night. The memory of the guilt caused me to pause. It prompted me to make a change that was a huge part of my personal growth and protecting my child's heart. The guilt reminded me not to project my emotions on someone else.

Now let's turn our attention to shame. The most shameful time in my life was when I became a new mom. Every action, every shortcoming, every failure evoked a puddle of shame that sucked me in like quicksand. I wasn't drowning in water; I was sinking in the sand. I had nothing solid to stand on. All the while, there was a rock right beside me that was going to rescue me.

I felt so much shame about not being able to breastfeed. I felt ashamed that I was afraid to be alone with my newborn baby. I felt ashamed that I had been given this miracle baby and didn't know how to take care of him. What kind of mother was I? I couldn't even be left alone with my baby because I was scared.

Unlike the guilt from unloading anger on my son, the shame started to suck me under the depths. The more I felt the shame, the more quicksand I found. Deeper and deeper I went in. And the Enemy loved every minute of it.

Then a really important thing happened. I stood up among all the church leadership and said I needed help. I was safe and my baby was safe—but I was not okay. I needed help learning and adjusting to become an emotionally healthy mom, and yet, during that season, I wouldn't have been able to tell you what that help even looked like. I just knew it seemed like I wasn't going to make it another day. The day that I admitted I needed help was the day that I stopped feeling shame. It was the day that I was proud of my struggle. Looking back, this is the moment that commissioned me to write this book.

I told the shame, *no thank you*. I decided it wasn't going to define me. The more I talked about my postpartum anxiety and depression, the less shame I felt. I wasn't covering it up anymore. Like bad acne, I was no longer slathering it with more and more pore-clogging concealer. It's like I had finally washed my face and was letting the world see what I really looked like, unfiltered. It felt amazing. It still feels amazing. Because the truth is this: when we slay the shame, the mom in us will rise up.

As I started to feel better, I was able to tell my story to friends and family. In a few short years, I was helping women in therapy sessions, although it first took a lot of work on my end before I was ready.

Please know that every time you share your story, you will feel a little bit stronger. Every time you reveal your struggles, you will take one more foothold away from the Enemy. Every time you talk about how hard this is, he will lose more of his bloody grip on your life. Every time you confess your weakness, you will grow that much stronger—that much more beautiful.

The fact that you are struggling with guilt or shame likely means that you are a good mom. So, you can say *no thank you* to what the world has to say about how we *should* feel about motherhood. You can say *no thank you* to what your family and friends have to say. You can wear the struggle like a badge of honor. I've never met a mom who didn't struggle. If there is one, then her DNA needs to be harvested and studied. Motherhood is hard. Own it. Then be proud of your lack of pride.

# ANGRY MOM

With all of the new emotions in motherhood, one of the ones that caught me off guard was anger. I'm typically not an angry person. Weepy, sure. Anxious, yes. But angry? That's not my default setting. Yet don't be surprised if anger sneaks up on you in motherhood.

Let me start by saying you're not an angry mom. It may surprise many of you, but anger is not a primary emotion. Anger is always secondary; it's always caused by another emotion. Anger is a symptom of a deeper feeling or set of emotions. But before we work on the primary emotion behind anger, let's take a look at the anger spectrum.

It may not feel like it, but we never start out angry. We start out feeling less-than, guilty, or disrespected. There are myriad emotions that all lead to the final destination of anger.

## The Anger Spectrum

Enraged

Mad

Angry

Frustrated

Resentful

Annoyed

Agitated

Irritated

Grouchy

For me, more often than not, my anger develops out of fear. If I'm driving my boys to school and another driver runs me off the highway, it wouldn't take long for me to see red in that situation. Of course, bad driving is infuriating. But it's not the driving here that would cause my rage. It's the fear I would feel when my sons' lives were at risk because of dangerous driving.

Tracking the causes of our anger leads to real solutions and understanding why we feel the way that we do. Ironically, the frustration behind not understanding the cause of our anger typically leads to more anger. And on and on that cycle can continue.

So the next time you feel anything on the anger spectrum, find a word that feels right for what else you're feeling. The anger often distracts us from the internal cause for our circumstances. It masks the true cause that we all too often forget to address.

## Emotions at the Root of Anger

| | |
|---|---|
| **Sadness:** disappointed, insulted, rejected, displeased, embarrassed, insecure, lonely, neglected, depressed, doom, gloom, mourning, miserable, sorrow, woe, hopeless, discontent | **Fear:** alarm, fright, mortification, panic, shock, terror, anxiety, apprehension, distress, dread, nervousness, tension, uneasiness, worry |
| **Shame:** guilt, regret, remorse | **Trauma:** wounds from your past that get triggered can come out as anger or somewhere on the anger spectrum. |

Over the many years in my career, I have learned that humans get angry when we don't understand our emotions. Feeling many emotions at once can also bring forth mild to severe anger. This is why it's so important to identify the primary emotion(s) lying beneath our frustration, irritation, or rage.

Start using this simple technique to track your anger. When you get mad—or even just irritated—ask yourself, "What feeling lies under this anger?" Name the feeling. Then deal with the underlying emotion. This is the antidote to anger. This simple tool can help you be a better coworker, a stronger sister, a closer friend, and a more patient mom.

# ANXIOUS MOM

During my long career, I've noticed that many people sweep anxiety under the rug. I often think they do this because they don't really understand it, or they don't think that it's real. Because they don't really know what it is, they find themselves wondering, *Is it a personality thing/illness, or is it just a normal part of life?*

Every human being who has ever lived has experienced some level of anxiety. Anxiety symptoms can present themselves in a variety of ways, but it is especially acute for new moms. Anxiety is the number one reason that new moms make that first phone call to me as a counselor. It's that moment when they feel like they can't breathe, when they feel like they can't take their eyes off their baby for fear that their baby will stop breathing. Then, before they know it, the room seems to close in and their heart starts racing. Their stomach flips and they start to feel as though they might not have what it takes to get through the next hour.

Worst of all, so many of the new moms I work with don't even know how to name their anxiety. The first anxious mom I ever worked with thought she was having a stroke. The second anxious mom I worked with wondered if she was developing a heart condition. Years later another mom described her mom anxiety as a thought so painful that she couldn't help from thinking it. This is one of the hardest things you're going to have to deal with.

I've talked to thousands of women who can't even define what anxiety actually is. So allow me: anxiety is a list of emotional and physical sensations that happen in stressful situations. Anxiety costs over $42 billion a year to treat around the world.[2] Anxiety has a real price—and that's why I'm talking to you about it. In this section I want to attack anxiety—no sweeping it under the rug or glossing over it. I want to equip you to name what you're going through so that you can attack your anxiety and not just let it happen to you.

Along with an actual definition, I would like to help you

differentiate between an anxiety disorder and simple symptoms of anxiety. The difference between anxiety and an anxiety disorder is the severity of symptoms and how much they disrupt a person's life. Anxiety poses a problem when it arises and there's not a real threat. It can lead to depression, relationship problems, work issues, health complications, and even thoughts of self-harm.

Earlier, I described some of the thoughts and physical sensations a new mom experiences. The following table describes the differences between the emotional and physical symptoms of anxiety and how they might present within the body and within the personality.

| Emotional | Physical |
|---|---|
| Feelings of impending doom | Nausea |
| Feelings of being out of control | Feeling light-headed |
| Feelings of dread | Heart palpitations |
| Obsessive thoughts | Sweating |
| Racing thoughts | Trembling or shaking |
| | Shortness of breath |
| | Tightness of chest |

An estimated 19.1 percent of mothers are diagnosable for an anxiety disorder.[3] Under that umbrella we include panic attacks, obsessive-compulsive disorder, and post-traumatic stress disorder. These are all types of anxiety disorders. We know that these problems are extremely common, and it has only gotten worse during the pandemic.

I have a client who has an obsessive fear of the stomach bug infecting her family. You might be nodding reading that sentence, wondering if you have the same issue yourself. In fact, I definitely have a minor version of this obsessive anxiety issue. Nonetheless, this dear client has realized this fear renders her helpless at times. A mom of multiples, she feels helpless in taking care of her family.

Stomach bugs have resulted in her twin daughters being hospitalized several times. For this mama, the stomach bug was and still is trauma.

So it's understandable why this obsession has at times caused paralyzing anxiety for this dear mama.

For this client, her emotional symptoms of anxiety are feelings of impending doom, feelings of dread of waiting for the next child to come down with symptoms, and the horrific racing thoughts that she's not going to be able to care for herself or her babies. She has spent hours of her life in the obsessive fear of all the what-ifs and waiting for the other shoe to drop.

Her physical symptoms are light-headedness, nausea (I know. Ironic, right?), shaking, heart palpitations, and shortness of breath.

Please hear me when I say, this mom did not choose her anxiety. And please understand this important fact: *anxiety is a state in which we exist, not an action that we take.* Worry is not the same thing as anxiety. Anxiety can be caused by worry. We know that every human being who has ever lived has experienced anxiety.

Now, most of us know that the Bible tells us not to worry—but anxiety itself is not a sin. The things that we do *before* anxiety grips us is where we may encounter some sin. However, I can't criticize you for your sweaty palms resulting from public speaking. I can't judge you when you are anxious about holding your crying baby. These things are normal. Our job is to learn how to deal with our bodies and minds and let God deal with our hearts. When we do this, we get through our anxiety to the other side.

Even moms who are not typically anxious have had anxiety. They watch as their baby sleeps, making sure their chest rises and falls. They feel like the world is closing in on them when they can't calm their baby, when they're so exhausted and anxious they can't fall asleep, or—like my client—when they are always obsessing and waiting for that other shoe to drop. But friends, I am here to tell you: *anxiety does not have to become your default setting.*

TRIGGER WARNING

Some of you may recall the research of Ivan Pavlov, the famous scientist and the father of classical conditioning and the creator of Pavlov's dog experiment. Through painstaking time and effort that involved pairing the release of meat powder simultaneously with the sound of a bell, he trained dogs to salivate at the sound of the bell even when the meat powder had long been eliminated. Over time, the bell had become a trigger for the dog that determined how his body would react.

My client who I talked about earlier had a list of triggers that drastically impacted her behavior, mood, anxiety, and body. She would avoid going to church if she heard about a stomach bug outbreak. She would avoid going to birthday parties if she thought someone might get her sick. She avoided taking her children into stores. She spent time googling every possible symptom that her children would present with. A cough, sneeze, or extra bowel movement could set her anxiety off. These triggers acted as her bell. In many ways, they became an obsession and caused her to avoid really living.

Now, of course it's smart to avoid things that can cause our babies to fall ill. I would rather have another C-section than another stomach bug—and I'm not kidding. It's good to be safe. It's good to wash our hands. It's good to not spread disease. But we can't live a life that only involves avoiding.

Now, please hear me: there are definitely times that we have to avoid what is triggering us. There is a time and a place for everything. We have to make decisions to stay safe. We have to stay smart. But sometimes being safe and smart means exposing us to the thing that we are afraid of.

My client eventually realized that her children had missed many birthday parties for years. They hadn't run up to a buffet and grabbed a cookie for themselves. They'd missed soccer practices and dance practices and playdates. Her children were missing living their lives, and in turn, so was she.

We can't avoid every trigger for our anxiety. And sometimes we need to endure triggering situations in order to get through our fear. Because, trigger warning: avoiding triggers often gives them too much power.

When we avoid triggers, our nervous system reinforces that this avoidance keeps our anxiety controlled or completely at bay. Our brain stores these interactions and remembers them every time a trigger presents itself. Then it reminds you to avoid, avoid, avoid.

The problem here is that our bodies learn to avoid triggers much like Pavlov's dog salivated at the sound of the bell. When the bell was absent, their mouths were dry.

As time went on, my client started to face her triggers head-on. She started going to the birthday parties and made it through dance recitals. Sure, she was anxious, sweating on that short but achingly long outing. However, once the forty-eight-hour incubation period passed, she realized that the worst didn't happen. She didn't get sick. Her children were okay. No one was covered in vomit. And maybe, just maybe, avoiding sickness wasn't the answer to curing anxiety . . . living was.

Living proves anxiety wrong. It says "no thank you" to the dumpster fire that is anxiety. Avoiding is not the cure to anxiety, but living just might be. I know it's not easy; I've been there. But don't give up. Don't walk in fear. Talk to someone about your triggers. Then decide to slowly allow yourself to experience the discomfort caused by your triggers. Decide to endure some discomfort to prove the fear wrong. Your body will take notice. Your mind will take notice. Then you will conquer these triggers, one day at a time.

ANXIETY AMPLIFIERS

After understanding your triggers for anxiety and depression, it's important to know what actually *amplifies* your anxiety. These are the things that don't just set it off but make the anxiety go from bad to worse.

1. **Caffeine:** Caffeine is a stimulant. And guess what stimulants do? They stimulate the nervous system. While it's not bad to enjoy in moderate amounts, one of the worst things to do when anxious is order that espresso.

2. **Lack of boundaries:** This includes not saying no when you need to. It leads to overloading your schedule, your body, and your overall bandwidth. If you're already feeling anxious and overwhelmed, maybe it's not a good time for your family to come to town for a visit.

3. **Staying still:** Any physical activity that uses both sides of your body is called bimodal stimulation (walking, swimming, dancing, etc.). When we do any of these activities, the brain starts a process that reduces anxiety within minutes. So, if you can, settle your baby in the stroller and take that walk.

4. **Trying to control what you can't:** Focus on what you can control: your budget, your water intake, attempts to breastfeed, bottle washing. Focusing on what you have zero control over is anxiety-provoking and anxiety-amplifying.

5. **Isolating:** When moms are anxious, they typically want to go into their room, close the curtains, and pull the covers over their head. But that is the worst thing to do when you're anxious. Make yourself get out. Go to Target. Stop by a neighbor's house to say hello. Don't isolate. Promise?

6. **Perfectionism:** Lastly, know that perfectionism worsens anxiety because expecting perfection sets you up for guaranteed failure. Give yourself permission to do something poorly. Give yourself permission to fail. In doing so, you just might succeed.

Now that you understand a little more about your anxiety and what makes it worse, let's take it one more essential step: let's talk about how to manage your anxiety. It's one thing to understand it, but what we really need are concrete steps to make it better.

## TWO WAYS TO MANAGE YOUR ANXIETY

### 1. Rate your anxiety on a scale of 1 to 10.

Any given day, on a scale of 1 to 10, we are at least at a 1. Running late for your pediatrician's appointment, spending time navigating family conflict and tension at the holidays, the fear of a car wreck—having some level of anxiety is part of the human experience. Every human being who ever lived—even Jesus himself—has experienced some level of anxiety. A 1 is normal. A 1 is expected. A 1 means you're still breathing.

But a 10 is obviously *not* where I want you to be. I want you to know yourself so well that when you wake up in the morning, you know on a scale of 1 to 10 where you are. Every day, I want you to rate your anxiety. Know when you're at a 4, or a 6, or an 8.

From working in crisis mental health, I've learned it's very hard to de-escalate someone who's at a 9 or 10 without medical intervention. I've seen the power—and blessing—that is Ativan and Xanax. These medications take our nervous system out of overdrive and let our body rest and stop working so hard. Of course, rescue anxiety medications can be abused. But they do have their place.

My goal is for you to put real interventions into place when you're at a 6, to keep you from moving to an 8. After 8, it gets hard to de-escalate.

I want you to know yourself so well that you are able to prevent your anxiety from getting worse.

I have really enjoyed speaking over the years of my career. I know that at any given speaking engagement, I'll probably be at least at a 4. But I'm determined that I will not avoid the thing that's making me anxious. And neither should you.

So, thinking about it right here, right now—where are you today?

### 2. Move both sides of your body.

Have you ever been so overwhelmed that you felt like you couldn't see straight? Maybe something triggered you and sent you right back to your cornerstone trauma. Or your anxiety made it hard to take care of your baby. Or you have a fear that gets in the way of waiting in the pediatrician's office.

But then, an hour later, you take your baby on a quick walk around the block. You come home and suddenly realize you are no longer overwhelmed by any of your feelings or worries. You unlace your shoes, realizing that things feel manageable all of a sudden.

That short walk was more than something to simply clear your head. It was more than calming yourself. It's bigger than what basic movement appears to have brought to the table. That seemingly small movement helped calibrate you and released you from some of your overwhelming feelings.

It's hard for me to ask a new mom to exercise. I know you're sore, exhausted, and possibly annoyed that I would even suggest this. However, this isn't about "getting your body back." This is 100 percent about getting your nervous system to calibrate. It's about *attacking your anxiety* rather than letting it attack you.

So when you're anxious, angry, sad, or scared, moving both sides of your body is some of the best medicine you can give yourself. Whenever we use both the left and the right sides of our body, an emotional cooldown begins. The nervous system is activated and this calms us. Endorphins are released and our brain releases chemicals that act as natural antidepressants and pain relievers.[4] Moving your body is literally some of the best medicine a new mother can take.

Mama, the next time you feel overwhelmed, stuck, or scared, take a quick walk around the block. Turn on some music and dance. Or, if you're too exhausted, tap your right and left hands on your knees. You just might end up calm and ready to face the problem at hand.

*

As we wrap up a difficult section on anxiety, I want you to remember a couple more truths. First, know that the better your acts of self-care, the less anxiety you will experience. We'll cover this more in chapter 8. These acts of self-care, or coping skills, will become your anxiety insurance policy and prevention plan.

When anxiety gets overwhelming, *change your focus to something you can control.* This could be organizing a drawer or editing a photo. It could be making a grocery list or baking homemade bread. Engage in activities that give you a greater feeling of control. A few weeks ago, cleaning out my fridge helped tremendously with my anxiety. No task is too small. Remove the focus from what you can't control and emphasize the seemingly small tasks that you can control.

There are so many new emotions in motherhood, but I want to remind you that it won't always be like this. In weeks to months, you will feel completely different, especially once your hormones rebalance. I know that you don't feel exactly like yourself right now, and that is completely normal. There are so many highs and lows, and you may feel an array of seemingly opposing emotions in the span of twenty-four hours, which can be absolutely exhausting.

But I want to encourage you to try one of the techniques that I've put in this chapter every day. Be gentle with yourself—I know it's not easy. But one hour at a time, one emotion at a time, you'll find relief in the reminder that your body was given to you by God.

The sun will rise tomorrow, mama. Never forget who's responsible for the hope in this promise.

## 8

# Ugly Thoughts Living Rent-Free

## *Attacking Intrusive Thoughts*

My sweet grandmother died a little over a year ago. She was a huge part of my life. The very reason I was able to go to college and had a prom dress was because of her, along with God's incredible faithfulness. She was fierce and strong—the absolute definition of beauty, inside and out. I miss her terribly. Even though she had just turned ninety, I could never have been prepared for the loss.

I was grieving. So, as I often do, I made an appointment with my counselor. I had come to terms with her loss. I could feel joy that she was in heaven. I found it incredibly healing to picture her holding the twin that I lost during my first pregnancy. It made sense—they were in fact both identical twins.

Weeks after her departure from this earth, I had one major problem. The thoughts—the ugly thoughts. Well, really one thought in particular. My struggle was this: I kept thinking of what was currently happening to her earthly body that she had left behind. This thought would distract me sometimes when I would try to go to sleep at night. I didn't want this thought. Like a really annoying song, it was living in my head, circling around—rent-free.

I didn't want to admit this to my counselor. I mean, who wants to own up to having such a thought? "Normal" people don't think things like this, right? I finally told my counselor. She was the first person I admitted this to. Then she did something that surprised me. She interrupted me, leaned forward, and gently touched my knee.

"Rachael, you've got to stop. That's an intrusive thought. Is that a thought that is *helpful* for you? Or is it a thought that's *hurtful* to you?"

Counselors rarely interrupt. We are trained to not interrupt someone who is sharing something painful. This was jarring, but for me to continue would have been damaging. It would have fed a monster that I didn't want to live on my back any longer. No good could come of me thinking these thoughts. However, even at this stage of life, I'm still learning how to gauge which thoughts are useful and which ones are not. I'm thankful that this is a thought that no longer lives rent-free.

My therapist was right to stop me. These thoughts weren't good, or helpful, or holy. For me to keep on explaining them would cause harm and make it more of a habit for me to succumb to. They were hurtful, wounding, and evil. My grandmother wasn't in heaven appreciating that I was thinking about what her earthly shell looked like. No good could possibly come from those thoughts. So I started doing exactly what that wise counselor said to do. I started saying "no thank you."

So what are intrusive thoughts? They are *unwanted*, harmful thoughts. They are negative. They can be hurtful or defeating. They run like an annoying TikTok video in our brains. Sometimes they can even be about harming your baby or harming yourself. Again, they are unwanted. Trust me, I did not want to think about my grandmother's earthly body. Many times, postpartum, they aren't rational; they are chemical.

Because I know to be careful to manage the triggers of a new mom, I will not give detailed examples of intrusive thoughts new moms have. But know they can be upsetting. In fact, simply saying that these are upsetting, unwanted thoughts just doesn't do them justice. They may actually be violent and disturbing. They seem to pop into your mind at the worst possible moments. For many of the women I have worked with, it can happen in moments when they are starting to make some progress toward healing, especially when they're bonding with their baby.

Most mental health research argues that everyone has had intrusive thoughts in their lifetime.[1] The awful thought of harming a friend when you'd never in a million years actually want to do it. Imagining yourself failing over and over again in a what-if scenario. Thinking that you can't take care of your baby. But thoughts are just thoughts. According to the National Science Foundation, an average person has about twelve thousand to sixty thousand thoughts per day.[2] Thank the Lord that about 95 percent of our thoughts are involuntary and subconscious. If not, I would have punched *a ton* of people, especially people in traffic. But I digress.

This is important: If a person is distressed or upset by the presence of a thought, then they're likely not going to act on it. A thought does not equal behavior. Friends, intent matters. Intrusive thoughts cause real damage when we believe that:

1. They are factual.
2. We will act on them.
3. We are powerless to control them.[3]

That new ugly thought, the one that doesn't help, the one that hurts—you know the one. That thought doesn't have to become a part of your thought photo roll. It doesn't need to join your story.

# TAKE A HIKE

Years ago, a client called me in a panic. She was a new mama caring for a three-week-old baby. After over twenty-four hours of less than one hour of sleep, she shared that she was having some intrusive thoughts—and they were ugly. She paused and then shared her intrusive thought of harming her baby. She shared that she would never want to harm her. When I did a full safety check of both her and her baby, she passed with flying colors; she didn't want to hurt anyone, let alone her daughter.

But this involuntary thought had convinced her that it was going to cause involuntary behavior. This image of harming her baby kept running through her brain like a movie on repeat. That movie kept playing faster and faster until she felt sick to her stomach. It had convinced her that it must be true because of how much she kept thinking about it. Though she didn't turn the TV on and press play, she did choose to binge watch the replay.

The more we think a thought, the more ingrained that thought becomes in our brain. Also, the more we think about a thought, the more our brain will default to this thought when we're stressed. The more we fixate on such thoughts, the more we integrate them. We let them in. They take up residence where they don't belong. Eventually, they can join in on nearly every aspect of our lives.

Think of it like this: My client again has the same intrusive thought. Historically, her brain chooses the belief, *I must want to harm my baby because I had that ugly thought.* Every time she repeats this thought pattern, this neural connection becomes strong and fast. Like an eight-lane highway, the brain wants to take this route. The more that she chooses this thought, the stronger this road becomes and the easier it is to take.

But in this case something changed for her. Something exciting. When the same ugly thought occurred, though her emotions stayed the same, she decided to take a new road by choosing a new *belief* in response to the ugly thought.

We decided on the new belief that she would use to respond to the intrusive thought. Her belief was this: *I love my baby and would never want to hurt her.* This belief created a new neural pathway. It took her somewhere safe and real. That eight-lane highway belief was only taking her to destruction.

Think of it like this:

The **highway** of *intrusive thought* leads to a *harmful belief,* which leads to an incomplete bridge over a vast canyon.

The **hike** of *intrusive thought* leads to a *new belief,* which ends at a charming five-star Airbnb with a hot tub ready to enjoy. Granted, the charming Airbnb required a hard, long hike, but it was worth it.

Just because the highway is faster doesn't make it better—or safer, for that matter. That hike leads to rest and restoration. The highway leads to destruction.

Keep in mind, this isn't easy. My client's brain didn't want to take this new pathway. The first time she said the new belief in response to the thought, it didn't feel natural or authentic. She said it felt "fake," even though it's 100 percent true. She had to force it. But each time she repeated the new pattern, it got easier; it felt more real. Eventually, the ugly thoughts went away.

\*

For over a century, scientists believed that the human brain didn't really change after young adulthood. Around a decade ago, we learned that the brain does and can change throughout a person's life span. This process is called *neuroplasticity*, a term that describes the brain's ability to adapt and change. The brain is an incredible creation; it can grow new connections and eliminate older, less helpful connections. This happens when the brain alters its synapses, or the structure between neurons. Our brain can change the way it thinks, reacts, and even feels. In short, the brain can rewire itself. This happens when we choose a new belief.

A *belief* is a thought that we adopt, a thought that we choose to let stay and live in us. Taking a new route to rewire your brain feels pretty uncomfortable in the beginning. But every time you choose a new path to an event or stimulus, this neural connection becomes a little stronger. Your brain won't want to take this route; it prefers to take the highway that it already knows, even if it's negative and harmful. The new belief is long and uphill. It's a hike. (Can you tell I don't like hiking?)

Then someday, in the not-too-distant future, that uphill hike, that rigorous terrain, becomes more and more beaten down. It becomes a path. Then a road. Then finally, it becomes a highway that your brain will beg you to take. So how do we create these new paths? Let's explore.

## STEP 1: EVALUATING
## INTRUSIVE THOUGHTS

In my career, I have seen intrusive thoughts grow tentacles into almost every aspect of a new mother's life. Her self-worth, her self-care, her marriage, her career, her body image, her faith—you name it and I've seen it. We allow them, like a disease, to infiltrate our thought lives, our psyches, our bodies, and our souls. They can take over by telling us that we are worthless, lazy, ugly, and useless. They lie. They cheat. They steal and destroy. Sound familiar? Good. That's how we will know that they are not here to stay. It's time for them to go.

Our thought life is incredibly important to examine. Our

thoughts are the framework on which our behavior and our choices are built. It's what kept us going through school. It helps us stay married and enables us to move on if a relationship isn't healthy. It's how we build confidence to keep trying to soothe our babies when it feels like nothing is working. It's what motivates us to keep trying when we feel defeated. It is what Scripture, blatantly and unapologetically, commands of us. *Our thoughts are the battle cry to one of life's biggest wars.*

Philippians 4:8 says,

> Finally, brothers and sisters, whatever is true, whatever is noble, whatever is right, whatever is pure, whatever is lovely, whatever is admirable—if anything is excellent or praiseworthy—think about such things.

While we *can't* control what random, horrible thoughts pop into our sinful heads, we can control what thoughts we *dwell on*. It was powerful for me to say that thought, once, out loud to a trusted counselor. And it was powerful when she told me that I must—*must*—stop those thoughts in their tracks.

Let me be clear: Moms deep in the trenches of depression or anxiety may be unable to remove the focus from intrusive thoughts without the help of a counselor or doctor. One incredible beauty of medication is this: it gives moms the strength to recognize the intrusive thoughts and gives them the biological advantage to tell the thoughts to go away.

*Tell the thoughts to go away.* This may seem like a pipe dream to you. Some new moms have related this technique to magic. They can't see past their own fear to believe that they will soon be strong enough to tell the thoughts that they are not allowed in their heads. To *command* them to leave. *Guess what, sister? It's not sorcery—it's science.* Not pseudoscience. It's both biblical and scientific. I'm so excited to teach you how.

First, we learn to evaluate the thought. We have to decide if it is fact or fiction. We have to decide if it is helpful or hurtful. Remember Philippians 4:8.

## WHATEVER IS TRUE

Is this a thought that is the actual truth? Is it reality? Do we have facts to back it up? It is true that I am five feet ten inches tall. It is true that I am a mom and have brownish hair. It is true that I weigh, well, whatever I weigh today. It is true that God is the author of all truth. It is true that our weapon against falsehood is the sword of the Spirit, the Word of God. It is true that Jesus died for you and me.

## WHATEVER IS NOBLE

Does it hold to a high moral principal? Does the thought promote what we believe as Christians? It is noble to give to the needy. It is noble to do good when no one is looking. It is noble for my husband to get up with the kids on a Saturday morning and let me sleep.

## WHATEVER IS RIGHT

This verse is referring to what is righteous. A righteous person seeks to be holy. To act in accordance with the law. To act out of grace and mercy. *An act that puts God first.* It is right to act out of a hatred for the presence of sin in our lives.

## WHATEVER IS PURE

Purity is the action of seeking a life as a redeemed child of God. Living a life casting out sin. Living a life seeking holiness. Seeking to be like him. To be one with him.

## WHATEVER IS LOVELY

This is a grand, beautiful, attractive, pleasing thought. A thought that has high moral worth.[4]

## WHATEVER IS ADMIRABLE

Deserving respect and attention. This thought adds, not subtracts, from your mental well-being.

## WHATEVER IS EXCELLENT OR PRAISEWORTHY

Deserving of praise. The ability to put a thought on a pedestal and say, *Hey you: you are good, and great, and deserving of praise.*

So let's evaluate my intrusive thought. The icky one.

- **Is this thought true?** Unfortunately, yes. Her earthly body no longer looks like it used to. Her heavenly one rocks, though.
- **Is it noble?** Absolutely not.
- **Is it right(eous)?** I would argue that it is not righteous to spend time and tears on this thought.
- **Is it lovely?** It is the opposite of lovely.
- **Does it happen to be admirable?** Nope. In no way does it add to my mental well-being. It most definitely subtracts. It creates a deficit.
- **Excellent or praiseworthy?** It is not a thought deserving of praise.

Now let's do the same for you. Let's pick a thought—a mean one. An ugly one. A disturbing one. One that's not helpful, admirable, praiseworthy, noble, or excellent. It doesn't deserve a plaque in a museum. It doesn't belong on a pedestal.

I know this may be hard. It may be scary. It might be a thought you don't like admitting to that lives rent-free in your head. But write it down, declaring that the truth will set you free.

---

---

Congratulations, step one, part A is done! You identified one. Now let's determine its worth.

| Is this thought true? | YES | NO |
|---|---|---|
| Is it noble? | YES | NO |
| Is it right(eous)? | YES | NO |
| Admirable? | YES | NO |
| Excellent or praiseworthy? | YES | NO |

## STEP 2: EVICTION NOTICE: HOW TO RECOGNIZE AND DEAL WITH INTRUSIVE THOUGHTS

I grew up on a busy four-lane road close to downtown Raleigh, North Carolina—not a huge metropolis but definitely a city. Now that I'm grown, I live on a quiet street where almost all of the people who drive by are the Amazon delivery truck or a neighbor we know well. But in my childhood home, we had a ton of cars and pedestrian traffic on a regular basis. Expecting to know everyone who passed through would have been foreign to me. Even now, it is odd to hear people say that they are suspicious of a pedestrian because "they haven't seen them on my street before." It never bothered me to see strangers walk by my home growing up—whether a mom with her kids or an unfriendly-seeming dude on a motorcycle. I didn't mind the strangers because they were just passing by. I didn't obsess. No one made a fuss. My mom would usually say hello while we were pulling weeds out of her flower beds. My brother and I got back on our bikes or we would go back to playing with friends. We were safe. However, what we didn't do was invite them in.

This is how it works with intrusive thoughts. The intrusive thoughts walk by as strangers who we can't trust. These strangers say some pretty creepy things. Something in our gut panics. But they don't get to stay. We don't invite them for dinner. We don't invite them to move in. Intrusive thoughts pose a threat only if we invite them to stay. If we engage intrusive thoughts, we only do so on the porch.

It's hard to accept that we can't trust every strange thought that enters our mind. But it's true. We have to set hard lines to decide which ones get to infiltrate our lives. They don't get to come in for coffee or tea. We certainly don't give them a bedroom to stay in. We tell them that while they are allowed to stroll by our home, they can't *move in.* Your house, your brain, belongs to the Lord.

> As for me and my household, we will serve the LORD.
>
> (JOSHUA 24:15)

These thoughts aren't allowed to stay, period. Never forget, your *house*—your mind and body—belongs to God. These thoughts don't get to take up residence in your home, your heart.

Take a minute and design your dream house. Come on, you know you've already done it a hundred times; you probably have a Pinterest board. Now imagine your mind is that house. There's the road in front. There's a sidewalk and a fence—however tall of a fence that you need it to be. Now the porch—maybe a big one. And the front door. The door shuts firmly. It has several strong locks. *And only you hold the keys.*

1. The stranger on the sidewalk: This is the ugly or hurtful thought that has popped into your mind. Right now, he is not living rent-free in your house. He isn't even on the porch. He has started to walk by. You see him in the distance. He walks closer.

2. We vet the stranger: Is she sketchy? Do you know her? Was she invited? *Is she there for a reason?* You evaluate the

thought. Is this thought helpful? Will this stranger help me? If your answer is no, she needs to keep on walking.

3. We decide if they get to stay: Do we invite them on the porch for just a while? Do we entertain the thought? Let them have a cup of coffee? Still, they don't get to come in just yet. Why? Because we just met.

4. You tell the stranger it's time for them to go. The stranger serves no purpose in your home. You don't need their help and it's not going to help for them to be in your house. *If anything, they may burn your house to the ground.*

5. They keep on walking: Really take a moment to imagine letting them walk by, out of sight, while you hold the keys. While you protect your heart.

6. You celebrate making a good choice for you and your house, serving the Lord.

Some hurtful thoughts have to be handled a little differently. Maybe the thought is trying to accomplish something good. Maybe it's serving a purpose but not doing a good job at all. For example, if we think we need to lose weight, it might make us eat less. But we all know the picture of a model on our fridge doesn't motivate us to eat healthy.

It's a great therapeutic technique to do this: Thank the thought for what it may be attempting to do. Is the thought trying to keep your baby safe? If the answer is maybe or yes, perhaps we talk to this stranger on the porch with a trusted friend or preferably a professional.

When we evict a thought—one that doesn't make it past the porch—we need to do another essential step. An eviction can leave an emptiness. So we must choose a new thought in a hurtful moment. We have to invite a new thought that will be helpful and not harmful. This thought needs to meet the criterion of all God commands of our thought life.

So let's look at the dreaded thought—the one that almost every new mom has thought—and let's evaluate it head-on: *I am a bad mom.*

| | YES | NO |
|---|---|---|
| Is this thought true? | YES | NO |
| Is it noble? | YES | NO |
| Is it right(eous)? | YES | NO |
| Admirable? | YES | NO |
| Excellent or praiseworthy? | YES | NO |

Before we issue an eviction notice for this thought, let's acknowledge what it's trying to do. Is this thought trying to motivate me to be a better mom? Are there things I need to do to take better care of myself and my baby? Of course, we could all say yes to these questions. But if the thought is causing us to spend more and more time crying on the shower floor feeling worthless, this is not the thought that will make you a better mom. Here's the one that will: *I'm becoming a good mom and I'm proud of how much I'm learning to do.*

| Instead of: | Replace with: |
|---|---|
| I'm lazy. | I'm tired. I need to have grace for myself. |
| My life is over as I know it. | This is a short and hard season. It gets better. |
| I'm fat. | I'm beautiful and strong. My body has done something incredible. |
| I can't do this. | God's going to sustain me. |
| I'm not cut out to be a mom. | I am cut out to be a mom because God says so. |

As I think through the seventeen years that I lived in my childhood home, I don't remember the strangers' faces. I can't recall names. I don't know of any harm that was caused—because they never made it past the porch. We kept that boundary firm. I encourage you to do the very same today. Evaluate each and every ugly thought that enters your mind. Decide which ones get to stay. Your thought life can and will heal you.

## STEP 3: KICKING INTRUSIVE THOUGHTS TO THE CURB

For the ugly thoughts, the ones that have been living rent-free for quite some time, I have a challenge for you, dear mama:

Take that thought and write it down on a piece of paper. Hold it in your hand. Write down on another piece of paper all of the reasons that this thought does not belong in your body. The reasons that it does not belong in your life. Take the ugly-thought scrap of paper and hold it while you pray:

*God, this thought is not true, noble, right, pure, lovely, admirable, or praiseworthy. I believe your Word when it says to not think on these things. I have demanded evidence and I have not found evidence for this harmful thought. So, Father, help me let it go. When this thought comes in my mind, help me choose one that is true, noble, right, pure, lovely, admirable, or praiseworthy. And, Lord, give me the strength to tell this thought to go away.*

Now take the piece of paper and (safely) destroy it. Rip it, flush it, burn it, bury it. Because that's how we should treat intrusive thoughts, like the garbage that they are.

# 9

# My Body, No Longer a Wonderland

## *Loving a Body You Don't Recognize*

Here we go. A Christian counselor's chapter on body image—not on it being a temple. After having my babies, my body felt far too saggy, baggy, and icky to hold up the stone walls of a temple. In fact, it still feels that way. But our bodies *are* a temple. We don't get to choose otherwise. And so, we have to find a way to love and honor the body that we have—even after it has changed in ways we'd never imagined.

Looking back, I was pretty cute during pregnancy. But I would have wanted to punch you if you had told me I was. I gained almost seventy pounds in my first pregnancy. I blame it on the fact that the only thing that seemed to settle my morning sickness was McDonald's chicken nuggets and Sprite. Thank the Lord for prenatal vitamins because my little baby wouldn't have had adequate nutrition if it wasn't for them. My hair was thick. My skin looked great. I had that glow.

I remember standing in line at Chipotle and people letting me go first. They would see my big belly and ask if I was having twins. (People, it's time to retire that joke. It's not that funny.) I would smile and talk about due dates and cravings if they would ask. I remember strangers giving up seats and holding doors. I got tons of smiles and kind nods. Even little giggles as my mommy waddle became more and more pronounced. It's like my odd shape had permission. The weight I had put on didn't need excusing. I had a license for not looking a certain way.

Then I gave birth.

Strangers and some non-strangers treated me completely differently. A saggy, deflated, balding mess, I was no longer waved to go first through the checkout line. Overwhelmed, I carried my son in the heavy bucket car seat as doors were no longer held open for me. I remember a recurring bruise on my forearm from carrying that bucket seat. It became like an unwanted tattoo of how different my life had instantly become.

Rarely did anyone give up their seat, even though I needed that seat more than ever. People didn't hold doors, even though my hands were now full. I didn't get giggles and compliments, and I had never felt so lonely and invisible in my life.

I felt like I had disappeared from view and my son had gained every sight line on the planet. I was nothing. I was no one. I wasn't even worth holding a door for anymore. Why? Because I was no longer pregnant? Because I have spit up on my shirt and new acne every week? No longer feeling beautiful was a major part of my dismay and my disgust.

God absolutely loves beauty. Consider his creation as evidence. Look at horses or flowers or the Grand Canyon. Look at Lisa Bonet, Taylor Swift, and Adele. He loves beauty. However, he doesn't love vanity. He doesn't love when we carry beauty as an idol.

A self-admitted lover of cosmetics and all beauty secrets, I am someone who likes looking nice. Put-together. That polished but not-trying-too-hard look. Still, I've fought my weight for most of my life. I did and still do get acne in my late thirties. However, the ugliness I felt right after delivery was unexpected. What's worse, I didn't just feel not pretty, I felt gross.

Weeks after delivery, I was waiting for a follow-up appointment with my ob-gyn. As the John Mayer song came on over the speaker—"Your body is a wonderland"—I looked down at what had happened to my entire body (hips, ribs, bruises, scars, tears) and thought, *Yup, my body is no longer a wonderland.* At least I thought it wasn't.

Although I didn't have a great body image before pregnancy, I definitely had my struggles. I have always been and still am far from perfect. But this was the first time I felt gross. The feelings of gross were demeaning, damaging, and I dare say, detrimental to my mental health.

Three days after I gave birth, I looked in the mirror for the first time and peeked under my hospital gown and was in utter shock. Seriously. I felt like Frankenstein's monster being stitched together with patchwork parts that didn't match. A few days later I stood in front of the mirror looking at my C-section scar and everything else that looked out of place. I wept, but I still wasn't prepared for the major mic-drop moment my mom was going to give. Like me, she had a C-section scar from many years ago. "I'm so ugly, Mom. I don't even look human." Without skipping a beat, she said, "Aw, baby, that makes my heart so sad, Rachael. You are beautiful. Actually, my scar never made me feel ugly. When I look at my scar, I am reminded of how much I love you."

Her scar reminded her how much she loves her children. Her scar told her what she was willing to do to fight for her babies. Her scar meant strength and resilience and sacrifice. After that day, I never looked at my scar the same way. It meant something different because God says it was something different. God was saying I was not gross—I was glorious.

# #NOBODYSHAME

In an era of calling out body-shaming and the #nobodyshame movement, we are in better times. Instagram influencers are being asked to remove Snapchat and TikTok filters from their posts. Live videos are getting more views than ever. People want raw footage—real, messy life. We've seen enough Snapchat filters to fill a lifetime. We've seen so many that we are seeing influencers lose their sphere of influence when they use them.

Body-shaming is something that we should have given the ole heave-ho to a long time ago. But getting rid of body-shaming isn't enough. There's a piece missing. This is about more than eliminating body-shame; it's about introducing body *gain*. It's about our body increasing in its intrinsic value because that is God's design. It's about loving and appreciating the bodies that we are in while working to keep them healthy and strong.

To start, I want you to write a thank-you note to your body. You can't cheat and write it only to thank it for giving you your child. Write it to your body *today*. Right now. Even if you haven't brushed your hair in three days.

> Body,
>
> I thank you that God gave you to me. I love that you're tall. I love that you can run after your kids if you need to. I'm so glad your knees work so I can get down on them and pray. You digest all of the food I eat really well. You allow me the ability to make funny faces, sing, and squeal. You are powerful and strong. You are just as you should be.
>
> I'm sorry for all the chicken nuggets. I was in survival mode and was just trying to not throw up all of the time. But I'm going to work on it. It just might be a minute.
>
> I will build my muscles back. I will get you stronger. Even though I'm annoyed that you didn't give my boobs breast milk,

thank you for my hands and mind that work so that I can pay for formula.

Body, you are not gross. I appreciate you. I am thankful for you. I will spend effort taking care of you, just as you, through the power of the Lord, have given me feet to walk and a voice to talk.

*The more* you appreciate your body and the more you love it, the better you'll value it and take care of it.

## WE'RE GOING TO TALK ABOUT YOUR VAGINA NOW

"After a baby comes out of it, it's called a vagina, nothing else." A character played by Chris Rock in the movie *What to Expect When You're Expecting* says this to impart wisdom to another dad. It got a cheap laugh from me; maybe it's the immature seventh-grade humor I never seem to outgrow. But when I later thought about this joke, it didn't make me laugh. It made me think. Then it made me kind of sad. It was a "haha, hmmm" moment.

This cheap joke was funny, but the truth was harsh. Is our vagina less valuable after we give birth? Less beautiful? Less sexy? Does its actual value diminish after we bring forth life? If so, why? Because it's changed?

So your flower, your birth canal, your hoo-ha, your vagina. This thing of beauty that brings forth life is moved and rearranged. The center of desire, pleasure, and your human sexual identity has undergone a major renovation. We must hold on and heal.

For a time, it is definitely no longer a wonderland.

The word *wonderland* may provide mental pictures of Disney World or Mall of America. As a thirty-nine-year-old woman, I think of crystal blue waters on white sandy beaches at an all-inclusive Caribbean resort. Wonderlands are for amusement. Wonderlands are for playing. Wonderlands are for enjoyment. But not immediately after a category 5 hurricane hits it head on. It has to close down for restoration.

We took our honeymoon in Negril, Jamaica. We went to a resort that we definitely couldn't afford without the help of some dear family. It was beautiful. We ate some of the best food I've ever eaten. We swam with dolphins. We snorkeled. We swam in caves. It was definitely a wonderland for me.

We always said that for our ten-year anniversary, we would go back to where we went for our honeymoon. I had always wanted to go back. I wanted to feel like a newlywed again. I wanted to revisit the place that had brought us so much joy and pleasure.

As that date grew closer, a quick web search revealed that our beloved small resort had been wiped out by Hurricane Matthew. The online photos were shocking. Our adorable hotel, my Grand Lido, was unrecognizable. It was reduced to a wasteland. Flooded, all of the buildings demolished. Plumbing jacked up. It was not the magical paradise that we cherished a decade ago.

There was a new company that built a hotel where our beloved one once stood. We decided to go back, even though it would not be the same. Even though it was an entirely different building complex, the land had stayed the same. The beaches and cliffs remained exactly as I remembered. The property was renovated, but the land was able to heal from the storm that had swept through. Not only was it renovated and healed, but it was actually better than the quaint little hotel we had visited in 2008.

Your baby isn't a category 5 hurricane. But giving birth is. Whether through C-section or vaginal delivery, your body just endured one heck of a storm. It needs time to heal. Once it heals, you can rebuild. Then you can restore.

The land healed. Your body will as well. And just as I joyfully rediscovered the familiar cliffs and curves of the stunning shoreline that had always been there, you will do the same with your body.

Your vagina needs time. It may need months, not weeks. You are allowed to take this time to let your body, and maybe your emotions, heal. In fact, sex is the only human need that we can live without. Along with God and your husband, your vagina, stomach, and uterus just did something amazing. You brought forth life. You sustained life. The storm has swept through. Now it's time to rebuild—after we close for renovations.

Labor and delivery nurses encourage new moms to not look at the damage down south right after childbirth. I 100 percent concur. The way it looks on day one is night-and-day different from day 10, and day 18, and day 40. It won't help you to obsess over this. It will help you do things to foster physical and mental healing during these months.

Regardless of how you deliver, you tear one of two places to get that baby out. Both are labor. You tear up here or you tear down there. Either way, our bodies change. Change isn't bad. It's just change. Remember that change can mean it will be even better than it ever was before.

*

I have spent almost twenty years in the counseling chair. I have met with every type of client you can think of for every kind of issue. I specialize in working with couples having issues with intimacy. I have spent years working with men individually as a part of their marital therapy, and I have heard people reveal the most shocking of secrets about how they feel about their spouses. One husband even complained that his wife didn't make homemade soup often enough. Some tell me they prefer her to be blonde/redhead/brunette. Some often wish that their wives would take better care of their physical appearance. Deep breath, sometimes they do wish we would eat an apple instead of Cheetos. Some wish they would work out more. Those things are hard. But in all of my years, I've never once heard a man complain about how his wife's vagina looks after giving birth.

Hasn't happened. Not even once.

I've heard them complain about every other kind of thing. But they don't complain about cellulite, or stretch marks, or her being fifteen pounds from her goal weight. Do you know why?

Years ago, my husband sat with me and a few of my girlfriends as we laughed about which handsome celebrities we like the most. From Hugh Jackman to Zac Efron, we giggled talking about each of our "types" as women. We tried to explain to my dear husband that some men are "cute" but not sexy. We women can acknowledge the beauty without the sexual attraction. Adam Levine was too "bad boy" for one friend and Ryan Gosling was too "vanilla" for another. "But Jason Momoa is too bulky for me," said the third.

My husband sat dumbfounded. "Wait . . . Wait . . . What is happening?" he asked. "So, if you find a guy handsome, that doesn't mean he's 'hot'?"

I have learned something important that most women don't know. Let me give you a big dose of freedom. Men aren't like us. Straight and emotionally healthy men are pretty darn simple. To them, we are one of two things: hot or not. It may be simplistic. But that's what makes them tick. Movies and TV would have you think that men rate women on a 1–10 scale. I have met a few who do. Healthy ones don't do that. The simplicity of how men behold beauty is a thing of beauty. You are a thing of beauty or you are not. They are sexually attracted to you or they are not.

In all of my years, I've never met a husband who wasn't attracted to his wife because of the appearance of her vagina post-baby. Truly. He wants you to heal. But the most important thing to a healthy husband is that his wife feels good about her healed yet renovated and restored vagina.

Regardless of how you delivered, initially sex will feel different. Things have shifted around in there—a lot. Your G-spot has moved. The anxiety around intercourse can make it difficult to relax. In time, things will feel normal again. You will feel beautiful again. Your vagina will find a new normal once you have had time to heal. Trust this sex-pert. You got this. Just don't give up. Don't stop trying. And keep talking about sex with your husband. Try new things. New positions. More foreplay even though you're exhausted. You'll figure out your new normal. And you will rediscover your sexuality once it reopens after a necessary closure for renovations.

## FIXING A BROKEN BODY IMAGE

Our bodies have changed in ways we didn't imagine. Just as our bodies had to change to bring us a baby, our minds need to change in order to bring us emotional health. Here are some steps to take to feel better in the skin you're in.

### 1. BUY SOME CLOTHES THAT FIT.

"I'll wait until I'm at my pre-pregnancy weight before I get some new clothes." I remember these words coming out of my mouth. I remember them being said by many dear friends. I also remember this not working for me to motivate me to be healthier.

Friends, your body has changed. Your ribs and hips have moved. Your boobs have changed shape. No amount of diet, exercise, or plastic surgery can restore your body to its exact pre-pregnancy shape. Even achieving your exact pre-pregnancy weight does not promise that your clothes will fit.

Choosing not to buy new clothes, even a few items from Target, feels a lot like punishment. Why in the world do we punish ourselves for doing the thing our bodies are designed to do? Pregnancy wasn't the most natural thing for me, but it was far more natural than wearing a crop top.

I want you to go buy a few things that fit. That are soft. That hug your body in the right way. The colors that make you smile. That show the color of your eyes. You don't have to break the bank. You can do this while keeping some items you hope to fit back into someday. In doing this, you're reminding your body that it is something of value. Doing this is much more likely to motivate you to take care of it!

## 2. WATCH OUT FOR FILTERS.

"I shall put no unrighteous thing before my eyes." It's crazy that we live in a time that our eyes can't decipher reality. We often can't tell what people actually look like. We spend so much of our time watching moving images, we can't tell what is real. It's a lie that we can't shake. A truth that we can't spend. A reality that is cruel.

So, please, I beg of you, be mindful of what images you are filling your mind with. Are you scrolling through Instagram looking at the perfect and perfectly toned mommies? Is this a righteous thing to put before your eyes? It is essential to evaluate what you are consuming so that you know whether it is helping or hurting you. For me, seeing the unending feed of perfect mommies right after they gave birth was harming me. Because that was not my experience having babies.

I did find a blog on real postpartum bodies. I had the dreaded "C-section shelf." The C-section shelf is when the scar is so taut that your excess skin just hangs over. Some people call it a "mother's apron." I don't know which name is worse. But this blog helped me know I wasn't alone. It helped me know that I didn't mess up, I didn't somehow click the wrong button that delivered me the wrong body. I had the body that I had. I had and still do have excess skin. I had and still do have stretch marks. But seeing real bodies anchored me to a healthier view of what this process is supposed to look like.

### 3. LIMIT MIRROR-CHECKING.

Checking can be dangerous. Sure, do the obligatory mirror check before a friend stops by—but don't linger. Use the mirror for what it is designed to do: show you the beauty that exists on the other side. It's not designed for self-hatred or self-deprecation. It's not designed to assign value. Mine is for appreciation of the beauty that God has given me, not for validation. If you find yourself obsessing over the mirror, set a timer and allow yourself five minutes to get ready.

### 4. DECIDE TO LET GO OF THE "TRIM TARGET."

I have a confession to make: I used to believe that if I achieved a certain body type and weight, I would finally be happy. I would be fulfilled. I would be enough. My husband would be pleased with me, even if I behaved badly. I would be happier in clothes, I would have better vacations, and I would even have more friends. I might even sell more books.

The problems is this: I now weigh less than I did on my wedding day. I achieved the trim target. Isn't that what all women want? To be smaller than they were when they walked down the aisle?

I remember the day that the scale passed that goal of mine. I thought there would be answers to questions that I had long struggled with. Life would have fewer struggles, and I would be instantly filled with fulfillment. I mean, I'm "thin-ish"—for me, that is. Wasn't that the goal?

Most women have a size, look, shape, or weight that they believe if they achieve, then their life will get instantly better. Let's acknowledge what yours is so we can address it.

This is the trim target that I have always believed:

---

I want you to come up with a real, achievable goal for your body. I want you to want to be stronger or to walk faster. I want you to feel good in your bones. Sure, you can want to fit back in your favorite jeans. But if you're a different size, maybe that's not a healthy goal for you right now. *Set goals that are achievable, measurable, and reasonable.* These are the goals that will build you up instead of tearing you down.

## 5. BELIEVE THAT YOU DON'T HAVE TO LOVE EVERY PART OF YOUR BODY IN ORDER TO LOVE IT AS A WHOLE.

As a woman knocking on forty, I have learned to love myself a lot. I like that I'm a good counselor. I like that I'm smart and quick-witted. I like that I love people well. But I know I can be pessimistic, anxious, and way too concerned about people-pleasing. Still, my drawbacks don't overshadow who I am as a whole. My flaws don't cancel out my general awesomeness. And your flaws don't cancel out yours.

I can love my face and not love my acne. I can love my body and not love sagging skin. I can love my shape and wish that things could be slightly different. It can happen, friends. Believing it is how you achieve it.

## 6. CONSIDER HOW YOU'RE EVALUATING OTHER WOMEN'S BODIES.

"She shouldn't be wearing that." "She should dress more for her body type." We may not admit to it out loud, but we judge others. We think about how a different skincare product, fitness routine, or haircut could be more flattering. I think that, ultimately, the more we critique other women, the more we critique ourselves. The next time you find yourself wanting to critique a woman's body, ask yourself: *Is this a godly thought? Will this thought build myself (and her, for that matter) up? Or is this negative critique going to add to the already toxic culture that requires perfectionism in women?*

## 7. RECOGNIZE THE BEAUTY THAT EXISTS IN YOU.

I still think one of the greatest singers who has ever lived is Whitney Houston. I remember I had her cassette tapes when I was a kid. I'll never forget watching her sing the national anthem over and over again. As a singer who's far from anything like Whitney, I was always afraid of my voice cracking on stage. One night in front of a moderately sized crowd at a voice recital, my voice did what I didn't want. That horrible, obvious crack came through the mic. I finished my song, which went beautifully. Days later, my voice teacher showed me a video of Whitney. She was singing, bringing down the house with that voice. But there was a moment when her voice cracked.

"Did you hear that, Rachael?" my teacher asked. I had to go back and listen to it again because her incredible voice and talent overshadowed her moment of slight imperfection. If Whitney had stopped that performance, panicked, and walked off the stage, maybe that's what we would remember that night for. No one cared that her voice barely cracked. She was Whitney. But if she had put the spotlight on her flaw, then we would have too. The flaw doesn't take away from the beauty that exists.

Before my musical theater and singer friends get too upset, I will never even whisper of comparing my talent to that of the late, great Whitney Houston. But I will liken my struggle with feeling beautiful to my flaws: flaws don't outshine beauty, but the movement of the spotlight to our flaws will.

We live in a harsh world, and people can be mean. There's no getting around that. My social media presence has revealed harsh comments about my appearance from time to time. I can't change that people have strong opinions about my face, my clothes, or my body. But I can change *my* opinions about my face, my clothes, and my body.

*

There's such a rapid change that happens the first year after having a baby. But we must heal emotionally with reference to how we feel about our bodies while our bodies heal. Not before, not after. During.

The stretch marks will fade. Maybe not completely, but that's okay. Your vagina may always feel and look a little different, but that's okay. Your hair will grow back. The skin will retract. No amount of plastic surgery will ever return a mom 100 percent to her pre-baby body. Your bones have moved. Even your organs rearranged to make room for your baby. You must find a way to accept that things will never be the same. If you cringed while reading that, that's okay. We'll get you there. But you have to decide you're going to change.

We have to learn to adjust to our new minds *and* our new bodies. Hair loss, weight gain, swelling, stretch marks—you name it, we have it.

You're not gross. You're absolutely glorious. You have done something that your body was made to do. At the end of the day, someone lied to you about your body, and that person wasn't God.

10

# Put on the Mascara

*Investing in Yourself When You Don't Know How*

When I was a little girl, my parents made a decision regarding my first big girl bike. This bike was going to be an expensive bike (aka a bike that was more than fifty dollars). Since money was scarce, it was decided that both my brother and I were going to help pay for our bikes. As I look back, I realize I probably paid only about twenty-five dollars of a one-hundred-dollar bike. But, to a nine-year-old little girl, that twenty-five dollars was a lot of money. It was an investment—a sacrifice.

Not long after getting this big girl bike, I was riding it home when it started to rain. I worried that it would rust. I thought of the smooth gears and pedals starting to decay. I knew I would never leave my bike in the rain. I thought about how I had carefully unloaded my chipped yellow piggy bank to give to my mom. How I had counted the crinkled dollar bills and numerous coins to make my "investment." It meant something to me.

I treated that bike differently because I paid for it. Years later when I was a new therapist, I saw a lot of clients pro bono. Actually, I worked for four years before I received a dime for my therapeutic services. (I can definitely say that therapists pay our dues.) However, even though I didn't make any money, it was important that patients paid *something*. One of my first clients, a teenager, paid $5 for her session fee. I didn't get that $5. Instead, it served as a donation to the organization for which I worked. It wasn't about the $5. It was about her being invested in herself. Because of this investment, this client took her progress seriously. She showed up. She didn't cancel at the last minute. She completed her therapy homework assignments. And she got better.

We value what we invest in. We value what we pay for. I imagine that if you happen to own a designer handbag, you probably take better care of it than the one that you got for twenty dollars. Your investment decides and determines what is of value.

However, investing in something doesn't mean it has to be a financial investment. Sometimes it's an investment of our time. Sometimes it looks like effort. Sometimes it looks like expending physical and emotional energy. But it is an investment. And investment assigns value.

Going back to the story of my bike—I treated this bike differently than I had ever treated a bike before. I never left it out in the rain. It always got locked up. My mindset of assigning value caused me to take care of it so it would last longer. In fact, I eventually gave away this bike in great condition when I became a young adult.

## SELF-WORTH AND NET WORTH

I have a confession to make: I have been known to roll my eyes when people talk about the role of self-care in mental health. My eyes come close to popping out of my head when someone in my profession talks about a new mom practicing self-care. But the thing is, it's so on point. There's often a reason a cliché becomes a cliché. Clichés can be a neon sign pointing to truth. However, before self-care can happen naturally and regularly, you must decide that you are worth investing in.

While I'm a thrifty girl, I am still learning the basics of finance. When planning for the future, one of the first things a financial advisor will ask you for is your net worth. A person's financial net worth is defined as "the excess of the value of assets over liabilities."[1] It's easy to calculate. You add up the equity in a home, whatever is in your bank account(s), and subtract your debts. Many people have a "negative net worth," which means they owe more than they have. I did for a long time. Maybe that feels like you today.

I believe we often use the same principle to calculate our self-worth. Even though we are *saved by grace, not by works*, we often calculate our worth by adding up all of our good works and contributions to the world and the people around us. Then we subtract our shortcomings, mistakes, and poor choices. I regularly meet people who claim to have a negative net self-worth. Their imperfections and poor choices outweigh the good that they perceive. In the same way, this is still something that I wrestle with in my daily life.

Though this method works in finance, it is not the way to determine our worth. God decided on our worth a long time ago. He decided that we were worth saving by laying down the life of his only Son. You are worthy. You are valuable. You may feel tempted to add your mishaps and imperfections and subtract them from your title of "precious daughter." Don't do it. It's a lie. We must refuse the lie and take on the truth. The truth is, you're so worthy that your worth can't be measured.

But the LORD said to Samuel, "Do not consider his appearance or his height, for I have rejected him. The LORD does not look at the things people look at. People look at the outward appearance, but the LORD looks at the heart."

(1 SAMUEL 16:7)

## FAITH IT TILL YOU MAKE IT

Perhaps you've heard the common phrase "Fake it until you make it."

I've joked that one day, years ago, I decided that I was awesome. I decided that I was worthy, strong, and smart. That, while I'm far from perfect, I'm a good friend and a great addition to any social gathering. I even determined that I was beautiful, flaws and all. I would tell myself that I was wanted and I wasn't in anyone's way.

But this security did not happen overnight. Even though I didn't feel strong, secure, and beautiful, I decided to pretend. But I didn't *only* pretend. I asked for help from people I love and from the God I serve.

I stopped wondering if I was worthy and started walking in my worth. The worth that God already decreed. The worth I was assigned before I was in my mother's womb. The worth of *daughter*.

It's time for you to stop wandering and wondering and start walking. Walk in who God has declared you to be. Start walking in the fact that you are beautiful, strong, and smart. Walk in the confidence of the strength that he has imparted to you. But also know that it's not fake. We don't have to pretend when we know the truth.

We have to *faith it* until we make it. It's very real, and it will set you free.

## THREE-MINUTE SELF-CARE

In my first months of motherhood, I struggled to take care of myself. I didn't yet understand the things we have talked about in this chapter. As a result, I wasn't sleeping, washing my hair, eating right, or wearing mascara. Unfortunately, the lack of self-care tends to make mountains out of molehills in our lives. Leaving the house with my infant son often led to me breaking down in tears due to the stress about packing the right things. The lack of control over what may or may not happen made me constantly anxious. I found myself fixated on the possibility that my new baby and I would ruin the atmosphere of a cookout or a hangout. It was a blender of anxiety that sucked me in and spewed me out into mush. I had no idea that my lack of self-care was impacting myself, my husband, and my son.

Like we talked about earlier in this chapter with my first big girl bike, we take care of what we value. But we also assign greater value to what, and who, we take care of.

Choosing to not leave my bike in the rain started something in me—something that was a little exciting. I would look at my bike in the mornings and smile. I remember making plans to save up for a basket to carry things to friends' houses. Technically, its financial value went down the more I used this precious gift, but I felt the opposite. The more I maintained it and fixed things that needed replacing, the more I wanted to stay the course and treat it with the level of care it deserved. Because I saw the value in reaping the benefit of caring for it, it kept me going. It impacted my decisions for years to come.

As is true for you, dear sister, anxiety is triggered and worsens when we're not practicing regular self-care. We're more irritable and less patient. We struggle to make wise decisions. Lack of self-care leads to impulsivity and behaviors that may be damaging to our bodies and minds.

Some people take a yoga class for self-care. Some people take long baths with bath bombs. Some schedule a mani/pedi or a massage. For many mothers and myself, there isn't time or money for these things at first. As mentioned earlier, my son's allergies determined the need for formula that cost more than our mortgage. We were going broke just *feeding* my son. So a massage was a pipe dream for me.

If you've ever met me, you know I'm a girl who loves her cosmetics. While I was in graduate school, one of my many jobs was working as a makeup artist. One thing I realized helped remind my body and soul *that I was someone of value* was to carefully apply mascara each morning. I would let my son safely cry (gasp) for just a couple of minutes every morning as I washed my face, brushed my teeth, and put on good mascara. I slowly separated my lashes and thanked God for all kinds of beauty and blessings in my life. It became a kind of ritual to me. It calibrated me. As small and seemingly silly as this was, this simple act established how the day was going to go for me. I would sometimes pray while separating my lashes. The rest of the day, I felt more human. At the end of the day (even if I had cried most of the mascara off), I felt more like myself. Even after being spit up on all day, I had still had three minutes to style my eyes. Applying mascara reminded me that I had not lost who I was when becoming a mom. Rachael was still there. And by taking care of myself, I gave me back me, a gift only I could give.

Over the years, I've heard some out-of-the-box examples of self-care. I promise, friends, we are not just talking about diet and exercise. Actually, even though diet and exercise are so important, let's set those aside for a few minutes. That is not what we were talking about today, at least not exclusively.

I had a client who would care for herself by organizing a different small drawer of her house. She discovered that this "sparked joy." Another client would sit on the floor and play with her dog. She would laugh when she would get that perfect spot on his belly where he would wiggle his leg. This helped her when she was feeling down. It's actually known to lower blood pressure.[2] One friend walks outside and stands in the sun. Walk through your house and open the blinds. Go outside and listen to the birds. Literally stop and smell the roses. There are so many ways to take care of yourself, even unexpected ways.

## UNEXPECTED SELF-CARE

As I mentioned earlier, it's important we understand that self-care is so much more than yoga and eating kale. And thank God for that. Here are some unexpected and underappreciated ways that we can take care of ourselves:

- organize a drawer
- pay a bill
- make a doctor's appointment
- compliment a stranger
- go to the grocery store for semi-healthy/healthy food
- text a friend
- return that thing that's been sitting in your car that needs to be returned
- read old cards and letters from friends
- look at fun pictures from your time in college or when you took a fun trip
- drink really good coffee
- pluck your eyebrows (just don't overpluck)
- work on your budget
- do your brain dump
- journal
- compliment yourself
- give your body a good stretch
- ask somebody to brush your hair
- brush your hair
- make a to-do list

- sleep
- ask somebody for a hug—a really good, deep hug
- write down your prayers
- listen to a podcast
- water your flowers
- pray
- ask somebody to pray for you
- remember that you're worth praying for
- remember that you are worth asking someone else to pray for you
- buy yourself flowers
- remove dead flowers (if you have dead flowers like I do)
- make plans for the future
- plan something to look forward to
- dust a shelf
- better yet, if you can, pay someone to come dust your shelves
- create a blog
- watch cat videos on YouTube
- deep-condition your hair
- write down what you're thankful for
- put lotion on your feet
- organize your vitamins and/or medicine for the week

As you read through this list, I pray that you see that you have so many options for self-care. Maybe, like so many mothers, you've been overthinking it. If you have three minutes, then you do have the time. Since most self-care is cheap or even free, you can afford it. What simple act of self-care are you missing in your day-to-day schedule? What small three-minute tasks could you add to your day to show yourself kindness and love? If your brain is coming up blank, now might be a great time to ask your Postpartum Pack for ideas and support to make sure these moments happen in the weeks to come.

# BOUNDARIES

My first son was born just a few days after Christmas. That year had been one of the worst flu seasons we had seen in a while. Being a new mom, I was very concerned about sickness.

Mind you, this was pre-COVID. People were probably less aware and vigilant of sickness than they have been the past couple of years. I remember having to ask people to wash their hands. I even set boundaries about taking off shoes when we would come home from the grocery store.

I remember one family from our community group wanting to come meet our new baby. My friend was just getting over being sick. "I'm fine," she said. "It's just a bad cold. I feel a lot better today. I know I'm probably not contagious. I really want to see you and the baby."

I said, "I love you, but I'd feel more comfortable if we waited a little longer. I don't want to risk getting us sick."

I felt like a jerk. It was just a cold. It would probably be fine. Why was I so worried? But by saying no, I was saying yes to someone far more important. I was saying no to a cold that could have made the following week even more challenging for my family.

Thankfully, my friend didn't think I was a jerk. She totally understood. My no was cloaked in love for my son. It was cloaked in love for her as well. If I had not set this boundary, she could have gotten us sick, and she would have felt pretty bad about that. As I protected her from that guilt, I also protected my emotional health.

Earlier in this book, you made a plan for all of your needs. In chapter 2, we talked a lot about how to make sure one level of the hierarchy of needs is met so that we can meet higher-order needs. Now that you have made a plan for what you *do* need, it's just as important to make a plan for what you don't need.

One of the most important acts of self-care is realizing and practicing saying no. When we say no, our yes will mean far more to the people around us. Drawing clear lines, setting limits, and voicing expectations are the way that we can live motherhood to the fullest. And by this, I mean setting boundaries. Hard, firm boundaries.

Here are some examples of things you can say to start setting boundaries today:

- That doesn't work for me right now.
- I'm not letting people hold the baby right now during flu season.
- Now's not a good time for you to come over.
- How are we going to split this cost?
- I'm not going to be able to make it, but how's tomorrow?
- I'm not comfortable with that direction.
- I need you to not do that.
- I'm not really a hugger.
- We can't lend you money.
- I don't have the bandwidth to volunteer at church right now.
- I usually delegate that to this person. I'll send you their contact information.
- Thank you for your message. I'll address that on that Monday morning.
- I'm on maternity leave right now. Thank you for understanding that I'm spending time with my family.
- I appreciate the suggestion, but I'm going to do it this way.
- No, thank you.
- No.

First, be proud of yourself for having the strength to take this hard step. You've started the race and you've learned the lesson. Now it's time to finish the race. It's time to enforce the boundary that you've set. Because boundaries mean nothing if we aren't willing to enforce them.

It might be time to leave the uncomfortable conversations where your boundaries have been violated. Maybe it's time to leave a party where your lines have been crossed. Or to take away the toy that your child has misused again and again. It's time to demand the refund you were promised. Or to kindly fire that babysitter who isn't doing her job. Or to tell a family member that you don't want to travel on Christmas Day.

Setting a boundary is a small step in taking back control of your life. Boundaries protect both you and your family. They teach your children how to set their own boundaries when they are older. Emotionally healthy moms set boundaries. Do you? If not, that's okay. We start today.

## OUT OF OPTIONS

The year 2021 was a hard one for my family. We had a death in the family and my husband was laid off unexpectedly at the same time. It was devastating to lose so much in the span of one week. This turned out to be anxiety provoking, to say the least. For the first time in my life, I started to struggle with anxiety. Granted, I've experienced depression and anxious moments. But this was the first time in my life I experienced panic attacks.

I remember thinking I couldn't afford therapy during that season. The moment that we got the call about the layoff, every extra expense was cut. I went into panic mode. I forgot all possibility that God was, in fact, going to provide. I had just recently made the plan that I was going to cut back my hours at work so that I could write this book. Then my husband lost his job.

But as God always does, he provided. *Great is thy faithfulness*, right? My husband found a job that was better than the one he had before. God provided time in my schedule that I thought didn't even exist for me to write. As I think about emotional health, as I think about why you need to be emotionally healthy, I can't help but think of my own story.

Like my past behavior, I went into "worst-case scenario" mode. I never stopped to consider the fact that we had little debt and a six-month emergency fund. I started assuming that my husband wouldn't be able to get another job. So all of my self-care ceased. *I can't afford a gym membership, can I? Definitely can't afford my own therapy.* (Super ironic, I know.) But, as my panic symptoms got worse, I couldn't help but face the reflection of my anxiety in both of my sons.

Within weeks of my anxiety worsening, my mental health was taking its toll on my sons' happiness. They both started to have some mild symptoms of depression. They were irritable. They showed little interest in things that in the past would have caused them to shake the walls with jumps and squeals. I had to face facts: I was not emotionally healthy because I was not emotionally invested.

I was no longer investing in myself. I was no longer putting time, money, and effort into self-care. I felt like I needed to do everything I could to pinch every single penny. Many people would say it's totally logical to cut back on extra expenses when your income ceases. But this budget cut had too big of a price tag. The moment my counselor looked at me and said, "I think your little boy might be depressed," I made a vow to never stop taking care of my emotional health. Investing in yourself instead of accruing wealth will lead to emotional health. In turn, this process protects your child's emotional health.

At this point, I did the illogical but theological thing: I put my family first by putting my health first. I worked out. I went to therapy. I took time away from work to go to Bible study. I took time to pray. I slept. I watched Netflix. Within weeks of my getting back to therapy, workouts, and working less, my boys were happier. They started sleeping through the night again. They showed interest in our bedtime prayers. They smiled more and acted out less. My emotional health led to their emotional wealth. I treasure it every day. *The savings account can wait. Our children cannot.*

As a new mom, self-care isn't optional. We cannot feed our babies if we are not fed. We cannot soothe our babies if we have not soothed ourselves. We cannot love our babies if we haven't loved ourselves. Self-care isn't a luxury; it is compulsory. You have to decide that you are someone who deserves investment because you are valuable and worthy. How you do this will lay the framework for how your child will care for themselves.

Self-care isn't selfish; it's smart. If you want to be truly emotionally healthy, you have to start doing this. *Today.* Start with three-minute self-care. Over time, the three minutes will turn into five minutes. The five minutes will evolve into fifteen. There will be massages and fun trips in your future, mama. These seemingly small acts of loving yourself will help you survive and thrive during and after this season of life.

So, friend, invest wisely.

# 11

# Swallowing My Pride by Swallowing a Pill

## Understanding Medication and the Science of Our Struggles

In the early years of my career, I was super skeptical of medication use for mental illness. I had seen medication help countless patients. I knew how it worked in the brain. I studied it for years. But somehow, even with all of that evidence, I still didn't really believe that it had the power to foster healing.

My sweet mother-in-law has a rare form of type 1 diabetes that she was diagnosed with at age fifty-five. She is, by the way, the toughest woman I've ever met. Her endocrinologist found that the best way for her to manage her diabetes was with an insulin pump. Once she got her pump, this girl rocked it. She stays very active. She manages her diet and takes great care of herself as well as loving and taking care of the rest of our large and growing family. Without her insulin, she would rapidly decline. She might go blind. She could lose a limb. Then she would slip away. It's a scary thought.

In 1922, Sir Frederick Banting, along with two colleagues, discovered and purified insulin.[1] Before his discovery, most diabetics did not live past a year after being diagnosed. When he was only fourteen years old, Dr. Banting had lost one of his closest friends to diabetes. He was one of the pallbearers at her funeral. He literally felt the weight of her death on his shoulders. This led him to pursue a career in medicine to research and find a cure for this disease.

But developing insulin was an ugly process. There was a lot of trial and error. Money was lost. People scoffed and gave up hope. There were experiments on animals and on people. There were failures. One might assume that there were some prayers offered by one of the researchers or the human participants. Eventually, on January 11, 1922, the war was won. We had a way to fight back.

I'm so thankful for medical science being the gift that it is. My "mama by marriage" would not be with us if scientists hadn't developed insulin. How different our lives would have been if Frederick Banting had not felt the weight of this death on his shoulders.

I have gotten to the point that I really don't like the term *mental illness*. It's kind of like calling a fractured femur a "leg disease." We don't need to put it in another category. The leg bone is a bone. Bones get fractured. Insulin works in the pancreas to help regulate blood sugar. Paxil works to regulate the neurotransmitters in the brain. The brain is a part of the body. Depression is an illness. It's an illness that can and often should be treated with medical intervention.

Think about my example of treating diabetes. I would be shocked if a Christian told my mother-in-law to throw away her very expensive and very necessary insulin pump.

"You don't need that."

"Don't you want to be able to say you can do this on your own?"

"Oh, ye of little faith."

"Don't you trust the Lord?"

"How's your prayer life?"

It sounds ridiculous, doesn't it? Take a moment and imagine that situation happening with one of your loved ones with a chronic condition where they need medical treatment to stay alive.

I do want to pause here and acknowledge that God can and does heal his people. We have a lot of examples of healing in Scripture. In particular, I think of John 9:1–11 where Jesus spits in the dirt, makes mud, and applies this holy spit salve to make a blind man see.

> As he went along, he saw a man blind from birth. His disciples asked him, "Rabbi, who sinned, this man or his parents, that he was born blind?"
>
> "Neither this man nor his parents sinned," said Jesus, "but this happened so that the works of God might be displayed in him. As long as it is day, we must do the works of him who sent me. Night is coming, when no one can work. While I am in the world, I am the light of the world."
>
> After saying this, he spit on the ground, made some mud with the saliva, and put it on the man's eyes. "Go," he told him, "wash in the Pool of Siloam" (this word means "Sent"). So the man went and washed, and came home seeing.
>
> His neighbors and those who had formerly seen him begging asked, "Isn't this the same man who used to sit and beg?" Some claimed that he was.
>
> Others said, "No, he only looks like him."
>
> But he himself insisted, "I am the man."
>
> "How then were your eyes opened?" they asked.
>
> He replied, "The man they call Jesus made some mud and put it on my eyes. He told me to go to Siloam and wash. So I went and washed, and then I could see."

Jesus didn't *need* the mud. But he chose to use it. Do you really think that the God of the universe needed some wet dirt to heal this man? The Bible is clear that the man was not born blind because of sin. He wasn't cursed.

The mud was a tool that Jesus used to demonstrate his power and his glory. The Bible doesn't say this man was weak. It doesn't say he had little faith for needing the mud that was provided by Jesus.

So, what if Zoloft is the mud? What if Lexapro or Celexa is what Jesus uses to demonstrate his power?

I know that in no way does the God of the universe need the help of medication to heal mental illness. God also doesn't need counselors like me in order to heal mental illness. When we receive medical treatment for an illness, whether mental or physical (they're both physical), we aren't discounting the power of the hands of God. We aren't abandoning our faith. *God is using the skills and tools he has gifted us with to aid in his mighty work to heal us.*

Maybe, just maybe, taking medicine is a giant leap of faith for you. The Bible never posits that it is an exhaustive and comprehensive guide for medical treatment. The Bible doesn't give us blueprints for building bridges with structural integrity. The Bible tells us how to live our lives for and like Jesus. The Bible teaches us about what this life is all about.

*

Recently I watched a documentary on flat-earthers. The term *flat-earthers* refers to a subset of individuals who believe that we have been lied to by scientists and educators about the world being round. They believe fully and firmly that the planet we call home is indeed flat. I watched the documentary with my jaw dropped to the floor. I couldn't look away. Every person interviewed used a similar reason to say that the earth was flat. "Well, look at it. It looks flat." They explain a worldwide conspiracy theory that, at best, is far-fetched. The reason for my hour-long jaw-drop wasn't because of their belief. It was because of the lack of proof for this theory. "The earth looks flat" simply didn't cut it for me. Laws of math and physics assert that the world must be round. We can look to about a thousand years of nautical history to rely on the fact that the world is round.

One of the simplest ways to know the earth is round is by watching a ship sail off into the horizon and seeing it slowly disappear, with the tops of the sails disappearing last. The ship wouldn't disappear if the earth were flat.

When I was at the beach after watching the documentary, I thought of the flat-earthers. My children were playing happily in the sand and munching on Cheez-Its. (I have no idea how kids do this, because *ew.*) I saw a large fishing boat on the horizon, and I thought *score*. Since physics was never a strength of mine, I was intrigued to test the proof with a simple field study with my own eyes. Here was my chance. Over the next fifteen minutes or so, I watched and waited. Lo and behold, very slowly the ship disappeared, with the very top of its mast disappearing last. I knew the world was round. I had always been taught the world was round. But it was different this time *because I saw it with my own eyes.* I couldn't ignore the experience I had with my own body. It was real to me now. I had a similar revelation when I started taking my medication. It was real because I was experiencing it firsthand.

*

On January 16, 2012, I started an unintended research study of my own. This was the fateful day that I was diagnosed and began treatment for postpartum depression. *My doctor said that meds are a must,* I thought to myself. *He's a strong believer in Jesus and an excellent health-care provider. I trust him.* He ripped that prescription off his notepad and said, "Start this today."

I swallowed my pride and swallowed a little white pill.

For me, taking medication was a pride issue. I felt embarrassed that I needed it. I mean, I'm a therapist, for heaven's sake. Aren't I supposed to be able to fix myself? But God let all my preconceived notions about medication crash like a freight train running into a brick wall. I was humbled. And I'm glad I was.

I remember taking that first dose, scared. Paranoid that I would have some rare reaction. I looked at it and said a prayer. I called a few friends who had taken similar medications before. I asked them what to expect. They filled me with confidence that I was taking the right steps for both me and my family. I asked that God would use this to help me.

For me, taking that little pill was a giant act of faith. If I had kept going, I would have been leaning on my own understanding. But I trusted God. I was choosing to rely on him and his plan rather than on my own strength. I wasn't relying on my own knowledge and skill set. I was relying on who and what he had placed in my path. I prayed, and down it went. I'm so incredibly thankful that I took that step.

A couple of weeks later, something happened. (Know that some people don't notice the effects of these medications until four weeks after they start them.) It wasn't magical. I didn't feel "high." It didn't take the hardship away. It didn't make me not feel things. *But the sky was just a little bluer.* I noticed the rose petals falling from the vase on my kitchen table. This moment reminded me of the dear friend who recently blessed me, and then I smiled. I started to make plans and look forward to seeing friends. I felt strong enough to take the next essential steps.

Medication is the life raft to our ship. Many ships never need to use them. But if they do, it's lifesaving. Because there's only so long that you can tread water.

As the weeks went on, I got stronger. I also attended regular counseling sessions to continue my healing. I prayed. I meditated on Scripture and leaned on some amazing old and new friendships. Before I had the medicine, I didn't have the strength to do the things I needed to do. I didn't have the mental strength to tell the scary thoughts to go away. I was stuck in that cycle of darkness. Now I was strong enough to do everything I would need to do to get better.

*

In 1633 physicist and astronomer Galileo was accused of heresy by the Catholic Church for stating that the earth revolves around the sun rather than the geocentric idea that was already believed. He was placed under house arrest for the remainder of his life. He wasn't allowed to teach the "heresy" any longer.

Now that we have more research, this may seem ridiculous to you. We know that the earth revolves around the sun. We don't question what has already been proven.

I don't question the effectiveness of penicillin. I know the power of Advil when I have cramps. Why in the world would I question medication's efficacy in the use of illnesses of the mind?

There are members of the Christian faith who do not approve of the use of medication for anxiety and depression or believe in its effectiveness. If you are one of them, please pay careful attention to this chapter. I mean no disrespect. I once felt this way, too, but have realized I was wrong. Is it possible you could be too?

Stay with me. Let's look at just one type of medical treatment for depression. The antidepressant Zoloft is one of the more commonly prescribed medicines for this diagnosis. This medication belongs to a class of drugs called selective serotonin reuptake inhibitors (SSRIs). I know it's a mouthful. Some other common antidepressants that are SSRIs are Lexapro, Celexa, Cymbalta, and Paxil. We know one of the main chemicals that helps us stay happy and hopeful is serotonin. Serotonin is a neurotransmitter, or a chemical in the brain that occurs naturally. Serotonin levels can vary wildly after childbirth. SSRIs help keep our serotonin levels *steady* and can manage chemical imbalances that could cause sharp drops in our mood.

\*

A few years ago, I had a new client sitting in my office. Her face was pale and her eyes sunken in. She looked completely hopeless. She had had a traumatic childbirth and now was facing the onset of severe postpartum issues. She was having thoughts of hurting herself and was afraid to hold her baby. Friends and family members had urged her to pursue prayer. She wept on my couch asking why God wasn't healing her from this infirmity. A few of her friends had told her that taking medicine for her depression was evidence of a lack of faith.

A few days later, this client started a mild dose of an antidepressant. Each session after that, she arrived with more color in her face. She seemed more hopeful. She started having the strength to stop the dark, cyclical thoughts. Though she still was struggling, she was no longer in deep suffering.

Within three weeks, she started to have an appetite again. She brought in her baby and we took turns holding him while we worked together. As long as I live, I will never forget the first time she held up her son and put her nose to his and smiled. A real smile—not an ounce of it was for show. It was a smile that happened seemingly on accident. She brought him back down to her chest and looked at me and said, "I think I'm getting better."

I know it wasn't all the medicine. I know it wasn't all the therapy. I know it wasn't just the increased social awareness and help she was getting from her community and her family. It was all of the tools that God has given us to treat this illness. She was starting to have hope. She was starting to become emotionally healthy.

It may surprise you, but therapists cry too. Though it's a rare occurrence for me while I'm counseling, my eyes filled with tears of joy as I watched her. My tears celebrated that moment when I found real purpose in my pain. I was able to use the hardship that I endured for this beautiful woman and her precious son. These moments are some of the most joy-filled moments of my life.

Not every new mom will need medication. But if you notice that symptoms last for more than a week or two, call your doctor. Start with your ob-gyn. This is very important: if you have had thoughts of harming yourself or someone else, you need to stay on your medication. I know I have said it earlier in the book, but if you have a plan to harm yourself or someone else, you need to immediately go the closest emergency room.

Think one more time about treating diabetes with insulin. Remember that diabetics would surely die without this treatment. If mental illness is just an illness, then that's how we should make decisions surrounding it. Sadly, some women suffering with depression and anxiety do harm themselves. Medication saves lives; I've lived it and witnessed it. It can also help you bond with your baby. If the issue was solely spiritual in nature, then medication wouldn't help.

He did not afflict me. He was anointing me. Dear sister, how long can you tread water? Aren't you tired? Who might you be weighing down by not accepting help? Maybe you were once blind, and now you see. Maybe you still need the mud, the life raft.

So, I challenge you today to consider that you might be done treading water. It might be time to talk to your doctor.

*

God has given us a lot of faith and a whole lot of science in the struggles that we face. I'm proud to be a therapist and to have a therapist. I'm also glad I took medicine for several years of my life.

I know that if I ever need that little white pill again, I'll be the first in line to accept that help.

In my career, I have had this feeling—one that weighs on me, year after year. It happens when I'm urging a friend or family member to go see a counselor. When I'm reinforcing that a client isn't ready to go off their meds. When I'm begging someone, mid-panic attack, to go to the emergency room or to call their doctor. For me, this moment feels exactly like when my babies would fight sleep. As I held them, I could see on their face the thing that they needed the most. I watched them struggle as they fought the very thing they needed. My heart has ached in these moments. I have felt beyond frustrated in these moments. So I've learned to do something with these feelings: I tell my client how it makes me feel to watch them fight the help that I'm offering them.

I don't do this to make them feel guilty or to manipulate or to make that moment about me. I do this to show them the depths of their decisions. The impact of their yeses and their nos. And to show them that someone cares about them enough to get frustrated with them.

Sister, don't lie in your Father's arms and fight the hand that longs to heal you. He longs to comfort you. He longs to give you peace. Don't squirm, sweat, scream, and fight against the rest that he offers.

Instead, lay your head down. Close your eyes. Decide to rest in the arms that are holding you and say, "Okay." Maybe the people closest to you (aka your doctor, friends, pastor) do want what's best for you. Maybe, just maybe, medicine and therapy will help. They sure did for me.

In short, if you need it, and if people you trust say you need the help, take the pill. Go to the counseling appointment. Sit across from a nice lady like me, and let us help you.

Mama, I know you're so tired. So let's get you some rest. Let's get you some help.

# 12

# A Soft Place to Cling

## *Bonding with Your Baby*

After giving birth, I kept waiting for that magical bond to show up like Cinderella's stunning ball gown and glass slippers. The problem with this image is I expected my baby to be the fairy godmother. That seems unfair because . . . he's just a *little* baby.

I wish I had known the truth. I was looking for love in all the wrong places. I was looking for my baby to show me love so that I could love him better. I wish someone had told me that my ball gown (motherhood) isn't knit together in colorful songs by adorable cartoon mice, birds, and a fairy godmother. It is knit together by the Lord and my willingness to seek him in all things. My "dress" would be a less perfect yet far more beautiful pair of leggings and a stained hoodie. It would become priceless, imperfect, and messy motherhood.

In this chapter, I'm going to teach you how to bond with and delight in your baby and point out all the ways you have already achieved both of these essential tasks.

*

It was a Wednesday morning in 2011. I was at the hospital in the early stages of labor but preparing for a planned C-section. Only a few days after Christmas, I had spent the previous days being monitored by family members who would jump and giggle every time I had a contraction. Though I love my family dearly, I remember wanting to punch them. Contractions are no joke, and I had been having them for weeks at that point.

The nurse held the back of my hospital gown together as I walked to the surgical suite. I remember being surprised how bright the room was. *Not at all like* Grey's Anatomy, I thought. I winced as I saw a long metal counter full of hundreds of sterilized surgical instruments.

"Let's get you up on the table, sweetie," the nurse said.

I flopped up on the cold surgical table like an injured manatee. The nurse lifted my legs to help me. Another contraction came. A lot of words came out of my mouth during this moment that I won't repeat.

"Alrighty, are you ready for your spinal block now?" the nurse asked.

I mean, I had to be ready, right? I was in too much pain to make my typical sarcastic joke of "Do I have a choice?"

I curled up my back and held the pillow to brace for what was to come. The nurse hugged me on the other side of that cold table and reassured me that I could do this. To this day, I can't recall her face or her name, but I'll never forget the sound of her voice or the smell of the fabric softener on her scrubs. I pray she reads this someday and knows she's still my hero.

There was a pinch, a stab, and then fire down both legs—and

then it began. They laid me down and I felt so sick. My husband appeared at my right-hand side and sat down close to my head. "You're doing great," he said.

My memories are fuzzy at this point. I didn't have any medication to dull my mental processes. But my concept of time started to slow down and speed up all at once.

What felt like minutes later they said, "He has red hair!" My husband bravely chose to stand up and watch them pull our baby boy from my body.

"Bend at your knees," I heard the nurse tell Mitch.

They didn't want Dad to pass out in the operating room.

The moment they pulled my son from my body, my body temperature dropped significantly—like when Aladdin was banished to the Arctic. I started to shiver like I never had before. The doctors and nurses assured me that this was completely normal. "We just took out your space heater, honey," they said while my teeth chattered so hard I feared they would crack. They put warming blankets on me and finished suturing my body. Unlike Aladdin, I couldn't grab Abu and hold him for extra warmth.

I spent the first thirty minutes of my son's earthly life unable to hold him. My husband gave him his first bath and held his face to mine. But because I couldn't stop shaking, I was unable to use my arms to safely hold him. I couldn't stop my teeth from chattering to kiss him.

*Oh no*, I thought. *He'll never bond with me.*

I remember lying in the surgical suite praying God would help my arms stop convulsing so I could hold my baby. My miracle son. I wanted to hold him in my arms and start the process of building a strong attachment. In this moment, I feared that I had somehow missed a pivotal moment that would be the cornerstone of my son's self-esteem and the strength of our bond.

It's a common belief that a secure attachment grows between mother and baby during the first weeks of life. Some will say that the first *moments* are pivotal to create that secure bond. If we miss these moments, according to some, we're just out of luck.

It is the notion that, immediately after birth, babies, like goslings, imprint or bond in a glue-like fashion to their caregiver, presumably the mother, and that birth bonding is critical. In fact, we now know that human babies' attachment does not occur all at once and does not happen just at birth. It is a cumulative process of minute interchanges between a child and caregiver over a period of many months, perhaps even years . . . . Key to attachment is the child's ability to secure a close and trusting, reciprocal relationship with one caretaker, male or female.[1]

The truth is, attachment grows over literally millions of interactions between mothers and their children. From the moment of birth, a baby is neurologically designed to engage his or her mother—from the first cries that prompt mom to come close, to the kisses on the forehead. Mom's soothing rocks, sounds, eye contact, smiles, and every other response build the attachment between a baby and his mom.

For longer than I would like to admit, I was convinced that I had "missed my shot" to bond with my son. I worried my precious window of time went out the window. Sisters, I am so glad to say to you something that no one said to me: If you are struggling, you have not missed your chance to bond with your baby. The time to bond with your baby is not a short, narrow window. *It is long and wide, full of grace, just like God's love for us.*

We get millions of chances to bond with our babies. Thank God for that. Building your attachment with your baby lays the framework for your child to build an attachment with God.

I'm so glad that I can stand on the other side of that first year—the fourth trimester, as many call it—and see the hope and resilience that has existed with both of my sons and with myself. I know you may not be able to do that today. However, let's decide that we're not going to give up.

## HURTING BABY

"Oh no, do you have a fussy baby? Or is he usually *good*?"

People often asked me this question when my son would cry. And, as previously mentioned, he would cry *a lot*. I remember thinking, *Why does he have to be fussy or good? Is my baby broken because he's crying?* I cringed in these moments. I know that these people were well meaning. They were probably asking whether or not I have an "easy baby." I would argue that there's no such thing. Did I mess up and give birth to a C-minus instead of an A-plus baby?

In the first weeks of my son's life, I struggled with the judgment that came with the name and label "fussy baby." This negative label did nothing good for me. It achieved nothing for my son. So, I had to realize that I didn't have a fussy baby. There was nothing wrong with my baby. He was just a little bit more vocal than some other babies.

I realized that he wasn't a good baby or a bad baby. He wasn't a fussy baby; he was a *hurting* baby. There is a difference between a fussy baby and a hurting baby.

*What's a hurting baby?*, you may be thinking. Well, it just might be a baby being a baby. The only way that they know how to tell us what's going on is by making noise. The very fact that your baby is being vocal and trying to express his or her needs is a sign of solid development. It probably doesn't feel like it when you're in the trenches of an all-night cry session. Note that as their nervous system is very new in its development, your baby will feel everything in his or her gut so much stronger.[2] While a little boy might have a gas pain like a quick pinch, for your newborn baby it can be quite painful.

What I've just described is a common therapy technique. We take one thought and we reframe it so that we can think about it differently. We assign that thought some other value so that we change the way we feel about it. I want you to do this the next time your baby is fussy or gassy or sick. If you can't figure it out, if you can't appease her with rocks, swings, feedings, and gas drops, what you need to do is look at her and say, "Baby, I'm so sorry that you're hurting. But I'm going to do everything I can to make you feel better."

And then guess what, mom? The next step is to pray. Pray and ask God to take away whatever is bothering your baby. Ask him to show you what's wrong. God's Word promises that whenever we ask for wisdom, he will grant it to us. We trust our gut and go to the pediatrician's office four times a week if we need to. I sure did.

## SOOTHING YOUR BABY

In my exhausted state, I remember crying to a dear friend on the phone and she blessed me with a little list. I desperately wrote it down and posted it on my refrigerator. I would look at it while my son was crying. I repeated steps one through six until one of them eventually worked. Please know that your baby will eventually tire. Every day you will learn more and more about your baby so that you can stay calm while you're calming him. They'll eventually calm down and look at you and giggle. What was so important is that I kept trying. And when I couldn't keep trying, I called for backup.

I will share with you six reasons that your baby might be fussy. Here's the list, friends. Here's the big secret; are you ready?

1. **They're hungry.** Newborn babies eat constantly. It surprised me how often they eat. When all else fails, look for hunger signs and offer them breast or bottle.
2. **They're gassy.** While they're so young, they can't wiggle

around and get their digestive tract moving. They are powerless and are relying on us to move their bodies for them so that they can get those bubbles out, one end or the other.

3. **They're tired.** They fight sleep. That struggle is real. Keep going, mama. They will eventually give in and go to sleep. Remember, you're the mama who doesn't quit.

4. **They need a diaper change.** Some babies are far more particular about having a wet or soiled diaper. One of my sons would protest if he was wet, and my other son was too laid-back to care. Nevertheless, check that diaper and make that a regular part of your routine.

5. **They miss you.** They want to be held. They need some extra comfort. They may want to feel swaddled because their startle response is upsetting them. They're used to being in the womb, and when their arms fly free, it feels very insecure for them. Learning to be a person is hard and scary work for your baby. I noticed my babies woke up more at night when I worked longer days. They seemed to want to spend that time with me. Cute, I know, but exhausting.

6. **They're hurting/uncomfortable.** Sometimes they're sick. Sometimes it's something small like a tiny string wrapped around a toe or a tag on their clothing. They might need to be swaddled to calm their startle response. Maybe that fleece sleeper plus a swaddle is too hot for your baby. Some babies are extra sensitive to these things. Regardless, these are all important in comforting our sweet little babies.

When we keep trying to soothe them, our babies learn that their life has value. They learn that someone truly cares for them. They see God's love through our exhausted attempts to calm them, again and again. They gain empathy through this process. In addition, you will be refined through this process. You need to trust this process and to believe that, yes, you can.

# A SOFT PLACE TO CLING

There was a groundbreaking study that laid the framework for how we understand attachment with babies and their parents. This study was completed by Dr. Harry Harlow.[3] His research was centered on newborn rhesus monkeys and their bond with their mothers. When the babies were born, they were separated from their biological mothers. They were then placed in cages with access to two artificial "surrogate mothers." One of the "surrogates" was cold and made of wire and harsh metal. It wasn't warm or soft. However, this "mother" dispensed milk for the babies. The wire surrogate could not be clung to when the babies were stressed. The other surrogate was covered in soft terry cloth and was warm. It had places where the babies could actually cling to this mommy. But this soft surrogate did not dispense milk. The researchers were shocked with their findings: the monkeys preferred the mother that was soft yet didn't dispense milk. And while their growth rates were similar, the study concluded that the monkeys with the soft mommy, which they could cling to when stressed, were far better developed.[4]

It still amazes me that these creatures preferred the snuggly mommy to the one that sustained life and nourishment. For someone who loves to eat, I appreciate that God made us for attachment first, relationship second. Our attachment to our babies will teach our children how to form relationships as a child, a teenager, and an adult. We don't have to be perfect. We don't even have to produce enough milk to feed them for a year or two. We just have to be there, ready to be a soft place to fall and a soft place to land.

They will need that more than a trip to Disney. They will need that more than organic produce. They will need *you*, mommy—a soft place to cling to when they are stressed or scared.

This is no small thing you've been commissioned to do. I believe that there is no greater calling in this life than bringing up our babies to love Jesus. To raise up souls who seek all that is good in this world. The task is to bring up a mighty, godly generation of believers in Christ. The Enemy seeks to kill, steal, and destroy. What better way for him to destroy our child's life than to completely wreck the process of bonding with our baby? He wants us to feel hopeless, insignificant, helpless, and alone. The lie that the Enemy fed me like Goldfish by the thousands was *You are broken and can't be fixed.* He wants you to feel that way too.

Take a moment to realize that you are holding the mighty future of the gospel in your arms. The farting, spitting-up, exhausting, adorable, sinful future of the gospel. You are holding a future prince or princess of the kingdom of God. It's hard to imagine a baby Billy Graham, Elisabeth Elliot, or Priscilla Shirer. But they were once babies—their mothers held them at one point just as you are holding your baby.

## WAYS TO BOND

I sat in my Bible study with dear friends of mine. One friend, a mom of three children all under the age of four, sat with her newborn baby. She leaned back on the beautiful gingham-printed floor cushion as she scooted over the car seat where her new baby had been sleeping.

"He's awake," she said sweetly yet sarcastically.

With her past pregnancies, she had struggled with PPD. In the past, she may have made a comment like this only sarcastically. Now she nursed her baby while covering his tiny head with the white-and-yellow-printed muslin blanket. Then she lifted him up to her eyes. She cradled his head on her bare arm. She snuggled him in a soft blanket. I could see the bond growing before my eyes. It was almost electric. It was what I had specifically prayed for with this dear friend. I had prayed that the bond would be strong and that it would grow easily. Defying all odds and what the statistics said, this mom has made it through the rain. She has kept the faith. And it has fostered a beauty like no other.

I remember talking to friends and loved ones at my baby showers who said things like "You will have an instant connection when you hold your baby" and "You will bond the moment when you feel your baby kick." But bonding with your baby doesn't always come that instantly or easily. Here are some things that I've found helpful if you are struggling to feel that connection and bond with your baby:

1. **Make feeding time truly special.** Whether breastfeeding or bottle-feeding, it is possible to make this time good for you. Not just good for your baby. When you feed her, get the softest blanket. Put your phone away. Turn on your favorite Spotify station. Make eye contact with your baby while you feed him. This will increase the attachment for both you and your baby.

2. **Talk to your baby.** It may seem silly and counterintuitive. I know that they may not understand you yet. But I found it really healing to start talking to my son. I would tell him that this was hard, but I would tell him how much I love him. I would ask him kindly to be willing to go to sleep. I would talk to him about what I was working on. I would tell him to not worry about me because I was getting better. I even started to tell him about my hopes and dreams for him someday. Babies understand a large percentage of language through reading our tone and word recognition by the time they are only nine months old.[5] So I figured that he was already a sponge and was learning every day how to understand me. It helped me. It healed me. And somehow he heard me.

3. **Smell your baby.** Take in that newborn smell. Put your nose on her head. Tickle his teensy hairs on the back of his ears. Take it all in.

4. **Sing to your baby.** The sound of your voice and the melody will calm you and him at the same time. Play music over your phone, and dance while you hold her in your arms. Let her hear your breath and smell your skin. Let her feel you delight in holding on to her.

5. **Read or tell her a story.** While rocking my babies, I used to tell them of all the dreams I had for them. The things that scared me about the lives that they would lead. I would read my favorite books. They learned that the sound of my voice is something of comfort. They learned that the sound of my voice is a way to regulate their nervous system.

6. **Pray over your baby.** Here's where I took all of those dreams from number 5 and put them into action. I prayed that my boys would grow to know Jesus at a young age. I prayed that they would meet women who live a life for the Lord and are kind to my boys. I prayed that they would become leaders in this hard world that we live in. I prayed that they would fight injustice and be brave, even if they are scared. I prayed that God would keep them safe and *surround them with favor, as with a shield.* But most nights, I just prayed that they would allow their tired mama some sleep.

7. **Use touch and skin-to-skin contact as much as possible.** Play with her toes. Put your ear to his heart and listen to his heartbeat. Rub his back. Rock your baby.

Take deep breaths during the messy moments. It's challenging when they can't tell us what is bothering them. And then those things can drive us to more destructive thoughts and anxiety. However, what I do know is that God is going to help you. I do know that there are some general techniques that you can use. It may seem all too simple. But we tend to forget that the simplest techniques can be the solution. So, let's go simple and let's solve.

# TRUST VERSUS MISTRUST

In the first three months of life, it is important that you attempt—let me say it again, *attempt*—to respond to your baby's needs within five to ten minutes. The first few weeks of life are the most essential. Dr. Erik Erickson, a pioneer in developmental psychology, studied the importance of this. The lesson a baby is learning during the first weeks of life is trust versus mistrust.

Let me explain. A newborn baby who cries out in hunger or pain or wants to be held is learning an important life lesson: Can I trust people to respond to my cries? Can I trust these people (typically mom and dad) to meet my needs? When a baby cries and a trusted adult does not respond, that baby will learn the lesson that humans aren't to be trusted. I don't want to trigger new moms, but the babies whose needs are never met end up with attachment problems and other mental health issues.[6]

Babies who are generally responded to in the first ten minutes of their cries develop into thriving, healthy children and adults. The concern here is when a newborn's needs are *rarely* responded to. I would dare to say that that's not you. Not even close. I would conclude that because you took the time to read this book. Even if you are unable to respond to your baby, you have recruited help to assist you. You will not scar your child for life by letting them cry for five minutes. You will scar them for life if you, or another responsible caregiver, do not respond to their cries, period.

## I GET TO, YOU GET TO

I hate to work out. There, I said it. I don't like to run, squat, or do anything that requires me to sweat and get out of bed early. But about a year ago, I started to view it in a different light.

I have a dear friend, a mom of four children. She homeschools.

She makes her own laundry detergent. She blows my mind with how much she is able to accomplish in her day-to-day operations. Due to living on a very restricted budget and schedule, she was unable to work out for years of her life. She wasn't making excuses. She literally could not work out with her schedule. There was no time left in her day, no money in her tight budget.

We were having a conversation that was hard for me. I felt defensive. Our own budget was tight, especially during that season. However, my budget and calendar were not stretched anywhere as thin as hers. In that moment I realized something: I don't *have* to work out; I *get* to work out.

I don't have to go to the store. I get to go to the store. I can more than afford to fill my cart with fresh produce (half of which will go bad before I use it). I've never not been able to buy chocolate. There's never been a shortage of cheese, even during a global pandemic. (Thank you, Jesus.)

I *get to*. You *get to*. You get to have a baby. You get to take care of this baby. You get to love this baby. Many cannot.

Let's pause for a moment and clear something up: This is in no way a guilt trip. I don't want you thinking, *Rachael's right, I'm so blessed. I'm horrible for not being more appreciative.* First, we are all blessed, because God calls us blessed, whether or not we have financial means in excess. Whether or not we have a baby, we are blessed.

But I want you to think about your baby differently. I want you to think about being a mom as a great privilege, not a burden or a curse. *You get to; you don't have to.*

You are a mom. Being a mom is oh so hard. But often hard seasons of life end up being the most beautiful ones of all. And it's incredible.

# 13

# To Have and to Hold

*Using God's Scorecard of Motherhood*

My grandmother grew up in a very small town about an hour and a half away from Dallas, Texas. Her family were rose farmers. They were sharecroppers in that they didn't own the land that they farmed. She was one of six siblings and was also an identical twin. She stood at only 4 feet 10 inches, but still, she was the toughest lady I ever had the opportunity to meet. She talked a lot while I was growing up about what her life was like as a farmer. Even as an elderly woman, she still had the scars on her hands from when she would prune and bud roses. To this day, I think about the stories that she told me and the wisdom that she imparted to me.

One particular story she shared with me when I was in college stands out. Though she had an amazing family, she had a strained relationship with her father. We'll never know exactly why, but she didn't like to talk about him. But this one story told me a lot about the kind of man that he was.

One day after she and her sisters had harvested, pruned, and budded bushels of roses, her father picked the most flawless, best-quality roses and carefully placed them in six buckets of water. She and her siblings were then sent out into the downtown area of this small farming town. They were placed at different street corners and were told that they could not come home until they sold every single rose in their bucket. She told me that at this time she was only five years old.

*Five years old.*

The sun started to set as she was able to sell a few, but her bucket was still not empty. She never made her goal. She couldn't complete the task to buy a ticket back home.

It still blows my mind to think about this little girl. I don't know if she stayed on that curb all night long, but I do know that she stayed until long after the sun had set. She looked down and watched her tears hit the beautiful, perfect petals of their best-quality, prized roses. The crème de la crème.

She didn't cry much as a grandmother, at least not in front of me. But as she told me this story, her eyes filled with tears as she recalled looking at the scars on her hands in comparison to the perfect petals on the perfect roses. I still wonder what that felt like for her. Five years old, hungry, scared, and alone. Worst of all, she couldn't go home.

I think back and feel frustration with her father, a man whom I've never met. A man who was a lovable grandfather to my mother. How could he ask this of a child? Of a little girl? Once I put the timeline together, I realized that this happened during the peak of the Great Depression. Roses weren't exactly a priority in how American families were spending their money. I'm amazed that she sold any roses at all that day. What good father asks this of his daughters? What good father tells his daughter that she can't come home without fulfilling a ridiculously unachievable task? I know that selling these roses might have made the difference between whether my grandmother would eat that night. Again, it was a different time and there were desperate families. But I still keep coming back to this: what good father denies his daughters food and safety for the sake of his own desire or ambition?

Then I had a thought, and it wasn't a nice one. It didn't make me feel warm and fuzzy. It made me feel sad. *Her mother let this happen too.*

We don't know all of the nuances of this family story. We don't know if she was aware of the situation. We don't know if my great-grandmother was under duress and didn't feel she was allowed to go rescue her daughter. We don't know if she was in fear of her husband's reaction to any defiance. I know it was a different time. Women had far less power and say-so than we have today. We don't know if she was unable to go get her five-year-old daughter.

But I do know this: Nothing—and I mean nothing—could keep me from running as fast as I could to snatch up and cling to my child, alone, hungry, and scared on that street corner. I would run until my feet bled and would die trying to get to my babies. That's what I would do for my children. *And that's what our God has already done for you.*

My great-grandfather is not like our Father in heaven. And for that I'm thankful. Still we chose to name our two sons after the men in my family. My older son, Hunt Joseph, got his name from my maiden name, Hunt. My younger son, Reeve Arthur, was named after my great-grandfather, Arthur.

At times, I've been asked why we chose these names for my boys. These names are tied to both amazing men and failing fathers. There is one big reason that we wanted to do so: redemption.

I believe my sons will grow to be faithful husbands and fathers. Both sides of my biological family have a pattern of generational sin in the area of fatherhood. My husband and I want the chance to break the cycle of failing fathers in our family line. I want to redeem the names Hunt and Arthur because God is mighty. And through placing those names on their birth certificates, I was able to reclaim them by the proclamation of God's redemption.

So, even though the scars were faint, I will always remember my grandmother's hands. The hands that spent the majority of her childhood tirelessly working land that her family never owned. These cuts were deep and never left her. But the roses they grew were prized, and her family was known for producing some of the best roses in the county.

That is how I feel about our babies. Of course, no child is perfect. But to all new moms, they're the best of the batch. They are as precious, delicate, and fragile as a rose petal. As I think of my grandmother, not wanting to lean the bucket the wrong way and bruise these precious petals, I see her struggle. I see her forming new scars while laboring at this seemingly unachievable and unending task for her father and feeling completely alone. I have realized that I, too, have lived in worry and fear that there's no one there to tell me that I can come back home.

Sisters, I know your precious petals are fragile. Being a mom will feel impossible at times. But you are not alone. You have not been abandoned to complete an impossible task. You aren't on that street corner, unable to go home, unable to eat or feel safe. You are home. You are welcome at the table. And your Father hasn't abandoned you. He is beside you, right now, while you are rocking your baby, while you are cradling your roses. He is going to redeem this season in your life. And he will walk beside you each and every step of these messy and desperate days.

## UNWORTHY

Even though I had always wanted to be a mom, I didn't think that I would be very good at the job. Dealing with infertility, I thought, *Maybe this is God's way of telling me I shouldn't be a parent.* Over the coming years, several other doctors would confirm that it would be very difficult for me to get pregnant. In my own way, I resigned myself to this. I started dating my now husband. From the beginning, we talked about my probable future issues with infertility. He loved the idea of adoption and never batted an eye at this obstacle to become parents. In many ways, the festering foundation for my baby blues and PPD began to take occupancy in my soul a decade before I conceived my first son.

When I got pregnant the first time, it was a miracle. We had been married for three years and we were ecstatic. Our moms' reactions were amazing. This was going to be the first grandchild for both of our families. On Easter Sunday of 2011, I handed my mom a piece of paper with a Bible verse on it: "Then God remembered Rachel; he listened to her cry and enabled her to conceive. She became pregnant and gave birth to a son" (Genesis 30:22–23).

You may draw the parallels here that I'm talking about two barren Rach(a)els getting pregnant. My mom's eyes filled with tears of joy and she hugged me. It was a truly happy day. I was on top of the world. God had heard me—he had remembered me, and he had allowed me to conceive.

For much of my pregnancy, I felt *unworthy*. So many of my dear friends had not been able to conceive. I had walked alongside dear loved ones as they experienced miscarriages and infant death. I had been told I wouldn't be able to conceive, and now I was pregnant. I had deep-rooted and long-standing fears that I didn't have what it would take to be a good mom. Did we make a mistake? What's even worse, did God make a mistake? I prayed, "Lord, are you sure that I am worthy of this child?"

## GOOD MOM

So, what does God say? The definition of what makes a good mother gets warped in our culture. I think of martyrdom. I think of a superhero mom who never makes mistakes.

I think of my mom, the fiercely strong single mom. Every morning, without fail, I would stumble out of my room into the dining room. She would be sitting at the end of our table with her Bible and her breakfast. Sometimes hours before my brother and I would wake up, she was seeking the Lord.

I watched my mom learn to unclog sinks and assemble cheap furniture herself. I held the flashlight while she waded through our flooded basement to fix the sump pump. She braided my hair when I was sick. She stayed up with me many late nights as a teenager when I struggled with friend drama.

Since I have become a mother myself, I have had to deal with the sainthood status that I had assigned to my mom and my mother-in-law. I looked at these unbelievably tough and kind women and thought, *How the heck can I ever measure up to them?*

While in the throes of the early stages of new motherhood, there were many phone calls to my mom. I would cry as I talked to her about the guilt I felt over my emotions.

"I never remember seeing you cry like I'm crying, Mom."

She busted out laughing.

"Seriously, Rachael? I cried, oh I cried. I just went in my closet to do it."

At this moment, my mom lost sainthood status. And that was a very good thing. Elevating my mom and other "better moms" to this unattainable status was unhealthy. It's often said that "comparison is the thief of joy." It's so true. The person I was comparing myself to had hidden her pain from me. She 100 percent did the best that she could. But in trying to protect me and my brother, she made a mistake.

*My perfect mom taught me that stoic motherhood was not sainthood motherhood.*

I tell parents in my office all the time that the goal is not for your kids to never see you struggle with negative emotions. It's okay for them to see you sad, angry, even depressed. Your goal is to appropriately show your kids how you deal with these emotions. Now that my boys are older, I certainly try not to let them see deep emotions or pain, but I don't hide them.

After my grandmother died, I went through a hard season. She was really my other parent. In our family, it was always me, my brother, my mom, and my grandmother. Losing her was awful.

My boys were devastated when she died. We had time to prepare, but on the day she died, I let them see my tears. I didn't run and hide. I told them, with tears running down my face, that she was with Jesus now. She had died. And I told them what my tears meant. At that moment, they were given permission to cry. At that moment, I started to teach them how to grieve.

## CONFIDENCE IN MOTHERHOOD

I once read that the key to becoming confident in any task is repetition, repetition, and repetition. Some researchers believe that most human beings can learn almost any task if enough repetition of that task takes place.[1] If the physical and intellectual capabilities are present, we can become confident in our ability to achieve almost anything. However, the most rudimentary, basic task seems daunting when it is new, when it is novel.

The problem with self-confidence in new motherhood is becoming clear to me: How do we walk in confidence in our ability to be a new mom when we've never done it before? No matter how many times we've babysat, watched a friend's child, or volunteered in the church nursery, the game has changed. We are rookies, and will make rookie mistakes. It's now *our* kid. It's an entirely different mission and a completely unique baby. And it feels like the crushing weight of this beautiful responsibility bears down on our shoulders more than anything else we've ever done. There is no repetition of being a mother until you've been a mother for an extended period of time. No wonder we struggle feeling confident as new moms.

I recently asked my Facebook followers to tell me what they believed a good mother was. I wanted to share some of the thoughtful responses:

- **Mom 1:** I read a book in grad school years ago that talked a lot about a parent's role in empowering their children. The older my kids get (and the harder it is for me to let them be independent in a world that doesn't protect them in any way), the more I seek to build them up in ways that give them confidence, courage, and resiliency as they navigate new and hard things. My desire is to protect and nurture but I think a good mom teaches her kids how to engage the world around them in a way that promotes their family's values and fosters opportunities for them to grow into their personal strengths & giftings.
- **Mom 2:** Has good instincts, puts their child's needs first, is able to also balance their own needs!
- **Mom 3:**
  - she cares. She is attentive toward the child's emotional, spiritual, and physical growth . . . doesn't have to be perfect, just invested.
  - what does she look like? As in what acts do you see her doing? Eye contact, tone of voice overall, watches her child and you can see her affection/pride/joy. Heck, distressed, tired, frustrated, worried . . . honestly, I think so many things make up a good mom. So many hats.
- **Mom 4:** More often than not, she is patient, caring, provides a sense of safety for the child(ren), puts in effort to keep them happy and healthy, sets boundaries within which a child can explore, shares wisdom when appropriate, strives to be an example, loves unconditionally.

I received a ton of emails, DMs, texts, and calls telling me what it takes to be a good mother. The thing they all had in common was that a good mother loves her children and never stops trying. I decided to ask God to tell me what it takes to be a good mother. His answer was really simple, and I was surprised by his response.

He said, *1 Corinthians 13.*

*Come again, God? Seriously, the wedding passage?*

We usually think of this passage as what is read at weddings. I had it read at my wedding. There are four Greek words used for "love" in the Bible.

1. *Philia*: the love between siblings
2. *Eros*: romantic love
3. *Storge*: the love between a parent and a child
4. *Agape*: the unconditional love that comes only through our relationship with God

So I broke down this passage thinking of the love between a mother and her child rather than the love between two rose-colored-glasses-wearing, engaged twenty-six-year-olds.

> Love is patient, love is kind. It does not envy, it does not boast, it is not proud. It does not dishonor others, it is not self-seeking, it is not easily angered, it keeps no record of wrongs. Love does not delight in evil but rejoices with the truth. It always protects, always trusts, always hopes, always perseveres.
>
> (1 Corinthians 13:4–7)

After I read and reread these famous words, God said, *Look again.*

Mothers should be **patient**.
Mothers should be **kind**.

Mothers should **not harbor envy**.

Mothers should **not boast**.

Mothers should **not be proud**.

Mothers should **not dishonor others**.

Mothers should **not be self-seeking**.

Mothers should **not be easily angered**.

Mothers should **keep no records of wrongs**.

Mothers should **not delight in evil but rejoice in the truth**.

Mothers should **protect, trust, hope, and persevere**.

Let's explore these together.

## MOTHERS SHOULD BE *PATIENT*.

What does it mean for a mother to be patient? I googled it and got this definition:

Patience is "the capacity to accept or tolerate delay, trouble, or suffering without getting angry or upset."[2]

It means that she's not always in a rush. It means that she slows down and helps her child tie his shoe when he is struggling. She is understanding when something is taking extra time. She doesn't get angry when her Chick-fil-A order isn't correct. She is able to tolerate delay. And, when inconvenienced and delayed, she is slow to anger.

## MOTHERS SHOULD BE *KIND*.

When my son was nine, there was a moment when he fell down two stairs. I had just told him he needed to be careful and watch where he was going. He didn't. So he bumped his knee while I was trying to rush out the door, already late for an event.

I wanted to fuss at him and say, "I told you to be careful and watch where you were going." However, I heard that little voice in my head (you know, *God*), say, "Be ye kind." I went to my son, kissed his boo-boo, and asked if he needed an ice pack. I told him I loved him so much and didn't want to see him hurt. Then I *kindly, not sarcastically,* asked him to be more careful and watch out next time he is rushing down the stairs. By my being kind, he listened. If I had corrected him first, he might not have been ready to hear what I had to say.

## MOTHERS SHOULD *NOT HARBOR ENVY.*

How does jealousy come into motherhood? Hitting this sin struggle head-on is the ticket here.

As I prepared for this section of the chapter, I first thought that there's not much to cover here. I mean, *who is jealous of their own child?* But then I realized something: what if it's not about being jealous of your children but rather about being jealous of other children?

Years ago, I was counseling a client, a mother of three. Her older child wasn't testing as well as she had hoped she would. Her daughter's scores weren't bad by any means—they were just thoroughly average.

This simply wouldn't do for my client. Even though her daughter was healthy and bright, she couldn't kick the envy. "My best friend's son was tested and is an actual genius. His IQ is off the charts and he's been nationally ranked." Now, before we jump to judge this mom, I've realized that the longer I've been a mother, the more I understand the pain of this moment. The envy of other children's successes.

Envy steals joy from a mother's heart. Whether it's the envy of a friend's successes or the fact that her seven-week-old sleeps through the night, envy steals. Envy leads to brutal comparison that distracts us from building up our children to be who they're supposed to be. Envy distracts us to not take joy in the tiny victories we face daily. Envy blinds us from the blessings that God has for us.

We, as mothers, should actively be aware of envy so that we live out God's vision for motherhood.

MOTHERS SHOULD *NOT BOAST OR BE PROUD.*

A good mom doesn't brag about her successes. She is cautious about bragging about her children and their accomplishments. She gives God the glory for all of the wins in her life. She is strong in her humility. She is proud only of her lack of pride.

Pride can take many forms in motherhood. One day years ago, I had a dear friend call me out, and she was 100 percent right. I yelled at my three-year-old son in front of a lot of people at a Halloween party. Sure, he was acting out. Swinging his arms around and accidentally knocking over a shelf of paper plates and napkins. But his actions didn't warrant the volume of my objection. Now, I do think that raising our voices has its place in motherhood. But my yelling on this day had everything to do with me being embarrassed of how the other moms viewed my mothering. I was worried they would think I wasn't a good mom or that I wasn't properly teaching good behavior. I saw my son's face, devastated from my response. He was embarrassed and confused by my harshness. He wasn't hitting or running in the road. No one was in danger. He hadn't called his friend a bad name. He was honestly just a kid being a kid. My yelling was all about my embarrassment, my pride. I learned an important lesson that day: *Good mothers don't wound their child's soul to preserve their own pride.*

MOTHERS SHOULD *NOT DISHONOR OTHERS.*

I am at the point in motherhood where my children repeat whatever they hear me say. If I want to share some gossip or pass judgment on another person, they hear it. Consequently, they have said things that make me think they are starting to judge others too. This hit me like a ton of bricks, and I realized something had to change.

As a mother, it is my job to not dishonor my friends, my family, my church, my community, my neighbors, and my children. I should represent them well to not embarrass them. I shouldn't bring dishonor on my home by poor behavior. I should be cautious about how I talk about their father, my family, and their teachers. I should seek to bring honor to my home.

## MOTHERS SHOULD *NOT BE SELF-SEEKING.*

I have heard that we should try to say yes when our children ask us to lie down with them before bed. We should cherish these minutes before bed and tell stories and snuggle up in soft blankets. We should pray with our children and sing bedtime songs and read stories. But by the time seven thirty hits, I'm usually spent. There are many nights that I just want to get my babies to bed so that I can flop on the couch like a bump on a log and not move for three hours. Yes, there are some nights that it's okay to give them a quick hug before bed and take some time to myself. But there are also nights when God says, *Rachael, go lie down with your babies.*

Lying down with my boys is not self-seeking. It's centered on building a relationship with my sons so that they grow to be strong, loving men. Solid motherhood is built with fifteen-minute moments that lead to strong children.

## MOTHERS SHOULD *NOT BE EASILY ANGERED.*

You might remember when we talked about anger in chapter 7. If you've forgotten, perhaps it's wise to revisit this topic. We are called to meter our anger so that we don't wound our children to preserve our pride. I will note that it doesn't say we're never supposed to get angry. Sisters, there are times when anger in motherhood is appropriate. But we should be slow to anger. "Angry" should never be our default setting.

## MOTHERS SHOULD *KEEP NO RECORDS OF WRONGS.*

Every day should be a chance to try for a fresh start. No record of how many hours of sleep we've lost. Or how many mistakes they've made. There are no report cards for the quality of our children. They're all blessed and a blessing to us.

MOTHERS SHOULD *NOT DELIGHT IN EVIL BUT REJOICE IN THE TRUTH.*

We shouldn't indulge in negativity and destructive conversation. A good mother seeks relationships that are healthy, honest, and not toxic. She doesn't stab friends in the back. She is cautious in how she talks about people, even if she doesn't like them. She is quick to stop gossip and tries to correct sinful actions. She does not delight in sin, nor does she show her children that she is complacent in her sin. She fights against being lukewarm.

MOTHERS SHOULD *ALWAYS PROTECT, ALWAYS TRUST, ALWAYS HOPE, ALWAYS PERSEVERE.*

Good mothers make sure that their babies aren't left alone. They feed their babies. They make sure to take them to the doctor if they are sick. They check their fevers. They order/pick up groceries. They protect their own minds and bodies so that they can take care of their babies.

MOTHERS SHOULD *NEVER FAIL.*

I was doing well with these "shoulds" until *Mothers should never fail.* Agape, or love that comes through the love of the Lord, never fails. However, even the best of mothers will fail. Even the ones who have obtained "sainthood" in our eyes.

For this one, we get a partial "get out of jail free card." Again, 1 Corinthians 13 is written to explain God's perfect love for us. While we are called to model our love toward other people after God, it is not going to be perfect.

In our humanity, we are absolutely guaranteed to fail. And just like my mother made mistakes, you, too, will fail, dear mama. I pray that my failures will occur in a way that my children can heal and move on. You probably won't wound your child the one time you should have had grace and you delivered a nonabusive punishment. But if you have a lack of grace for your children again and again and again, the outcome will be different.

So, my friend, you will punish when you should have offered grace. You will have mercy when you should have punished. You will let them cry too long or too short. You will feed them food that upsets their tummy. You will get frustrated with your children more times than you can count. You will fail. The goal isn't to not fail. The goal is to make a promise that you will not stop trying to succeed.

I pray that you will be relentless in your quest to follow Jesus and to be a great mother. You will promise to not give up. But in your fight against perfectionism, you need to realize that we will all fail our children in some capacity.

## TILL ADULTHOOD DO US PART

Like my earlier example, we hear these words and we typically think of one thing: weddings. We think of the words we say to each other on a special day of our lives. But these aren't just words—they're vows. A vow is a promise that is made between you and the Lord. Maybe baby dedications should have more pomp and circumstance than they are usually given. We are making big vows the day we become parents. We're making bigger vows the day we dedicate them to God.

Technically, when we state these vows at our weddings, we are acknowledging that this is going to be a tough process. We are setting an expectation that it's going to be hard. We can promise that we will have sickness. There will be times of plenty and times of want. On my wedding day, I made that vow to God as well as to Mitch. I looked at Mitch and made the promise to him. The vow is a contract that holds weight and accountability.

Why don't we make vows for our children? Is it because "Until death do us part" isn't relevant to being a parent? It is true that we have our children in order to someday give them away. Just as Abraham offered Isaac to God, we are called to do the same with our babies. But there is a vow that we must make to the Lord. This is a vow to work hard to become the mothers we're supposed to be.

## The Motherhood Vow

I _____ take you _____ as my son/daughter. I promise to learn to be patient. I promise to pray against jealousy or envy. I will seek God daily to not be proud or to boast. I will work to bring honor to your name and to our family. I will work on my wounds and my frustrations so that I can be slow to anger. I will not keep a record of your wrongdoings. I will seek to delight in all that is good and rejoice in the truth. I promise you I will do everything I humanly can to protect you and to build trust and hope in you.

And when I want to give up or give in, I promise I won't. I promise to persevere to be the mom that you're going to need.

I promise that I will fail you. But I promise that I will work to not fail you over and over again. I promise that I will not be too proud to fix my mistakes. I promise to be willing to work on myself. I promise that I will stay in community with other believers who will hold me accountable. I promise that if my emotions get the best of me, I will seek help from others. I promise that I will make my relationship with your dad a high priority so that we can coparent and take great care of you.

Sister, I pray you speak these words out loud. I pray you share this with a close friend or family member. This is a beautiful moment, to declare a solemn vow that is rooted in God's promises over your child and over your mothering process.

14

# A Mom Who Doesn't Quit

*Measuring Your Emotional Health*

It's so easy to get knocked down or to get discouraged with a hard day. Because of that, it's essential that you measure how far you've come and celebrate it. *Remember, this is a marathon, not a sprint.* This is the part of the book where we will talk about how to measure your progress and how to keep going until the finish line. No marathon runner becomes one overnight. They start with one mile at a time. They celebrate their progress. Celebrating the first 5k is how they eventually run the whole marathon.

How much do you cry every day? (Note, I didn't ask whether you cried each day.) Not feeling your pain isn't the goal. *Knowing what to do with the pain is the goal.*

First, like we did in chapter 7, I want you to rate your daily anxiety and depression on a scale of 1 to 10 to track your progress. We are going to practice quick and simple journaling prompts to

191

complete so that you can know you are improving and growing. Clinging to God and the hope that is in his healing needs to be a major focus, mama.

One thing I can talk to you about today is balance. Man, oh man, does balance matter. The balance of work, the balance of motherhood, the balance of taking care of yourself, the balance of going to church, the balance of having time with friends, the balance of everything. *Everything.*

How do we find that balance? How do we know when we've struck that level? Let's figure that out together today.

We'll start with calculating a baseline of where you're at emotionally, right now. And we're going to do that with a very simple yet important number—a measurement called the *postpartum index.*

Here's how you figure out your postpartum index: Every day for the next fourteen days, I want you to evaluate your mood on a scale of 1 to 10. If 10 is the worst you've ever felt in your life (the saddest, the most anxious) and 1 is the best you've ever felt (the most elated, the most joyful), where are you today? For some of you, maybe your wedding day was a 1. For others, maybe the day you found out you were pregnant with a baby was a 1. Maybe some of you don't feel like you've actually ever experienced a true 1, and some could definitely argue a 1 is only heaven. In this case, work with whatever you have.

Now let's decide, where is your 10? What moment do you consider the absolute lowest moment of your life? Try to not linger too long in this memory. I know this could be a trigger, and I don't want to trigger you—but I do want to help you. For me, one of my lowest moments was when I put my infant son down in his crib after he had been crying for sixteen hours. Then I yelled at him. I demanded to know, "Why are you crying? Why won't you stop?" And then I had that thought: *What kind of mother yells at her newborn baby?*

That was one of my darkest moments. That was a 10 on a scale of 1 to 10. What is yours? What's your darkest moment? Maybe it has nothing to do with your new baby. Maybe it's that time you went through that awful breakup. Maybe it's that time that a parent walked out on you or when a trusted friend betrayed you. The important thing here is that there is no right or wrong answer. The important thing is to use the thought that popped into your mind—the first one—and try not to read into it too much. But let's take your darkest moment and measure it against your mountaintop moment.

Where are you on most days? Take those numbers from the last fourteen days and calculate your average.

Day 1 _____
Day 2 _____
Day 3 _____
Day 4 _____
Day 5 _____
Day 6 _____
Day 7 _____
Day 8 _____
Day 9 _____
Day 10 _____
Day 11 _____
Day 12 _____
Day 13 _____
Day 14 _____

Add this column up and list the total here _____
divide by 14 = _____
Days 1–14 Total Postpartum Index

This is how we will measure your progress. This is one of many ways that we can measure and make benchmarks to be able to see how you're doing at being emotionally well. As this number gets *smaller and smaller*, I want you to see the giant strides you are making. I want you to see that you're getting faster and stronger each day. I want you to see that you're slower to anger and more patient than you were weeks ago. I want you to know that you're getting better at soothing your baby, even though it may not feel that way. I want you to see that you have what it takes to do this. I want you to see that you're learning to soothe yourself.

*Accepting that you struggle to soothe your baby deserves a parade.*

So, about the above statement: I think I "wordsmithed" it for thirty minutes. Initially, I think I said, "Accepting that you stink at soothing your baby deserves a party." However, I felt like the above statement might be a little less harsh. You don't suck at soothing your baby; the baby's being a baby. It's what they're good at. We don't speak "baby," and they can't form words yet. If you dropped me in a foreign country where I've never heard a single word of the native language, it would be hard to survive. Like I say over and over again, did you feed your baby? Did you eat today? That's a win when you don't speak the language in a foreign country. We can't expect to learn our baby's language overnight. It's a long and steady process that yields confidence and stability in motherhood.

## HOW DO I KNOW IF I'M EMOTIONALLY HEALTHY?

It can be a hard thing to gauge. What's the goal? How do we know that we're getting close to our mark? Here are ways to know you are getting on track toward wellness. Keep in mind, there is always room to grow. But let me share a few signs of emotionally healthy people.

## 1. THEY HAVE THINGS TO LOOK FORWARD TO. AND IF THEY DON'T, THEY TAKE CHARGE AND SCHEDULE SOME.

I once read that to be truly happy, we need "something to do, something to love, and something to look forward to."[1] Human beings need to have things to look forward to. It's somehow our default setting. We need these things to keep going during the hard times.

Sometimes it's a phone call with a friend. Sometimes it's a cookout. Some people (not me) look forward to a good workout. We all will come up short in certain times in our lives with regards to having things to look forward to. However, emotionally healthy people recognize the deficit and take control of the situation. They take control of their lives. They schedule a dinner. They host a game night. They make the phone call. They buy the Slip 'N Slide. They don't just wait for something good to happen in their lives; they make good things happen in their lives when they can.

It can be challenging for a new mom to schedule things to look forward to. We see our lives as an endless milk-making process along with "breaks" for washing bottles and breast pumps.

You may not realize it, but your baby is meant to eventually learn to be cared for by someone else, even in small increments. Even for an hour at a time while you wander an antique store or go get coffee and read a book. Even in the first months, schedule these breaks and they will function as flashlights in the darkness to guide your joy and happiness. They reveal the presence of the light at the end of the tunnel. These mini-sabbaticals will grow as your baby grows. I promise, there is much to look forward to.

If you find yourself with nothing on your schedule to look forward to, are you willing to go out and take ownership of your mental health and make it happen? When you are feeling down and blue, will you schedule something to look forward to? Will you schedule a trip to the mountains? Will you make some dinner plans at that restaurant you've been wanting to go to?

## 2. THEY DON'T BLAME ALL OF THE NEGATIVE CIRCUMSTANCES AND EXPERIENCES ON EXTERNAL FACTORS.

When I meet with a new client, I'm screening for many things. I'm wanting to know if they have a history of psychiatric hospitalizations. I'm documenting their medical history and family history. I want to know about any history of alcohol or drug abuse. There are many things that therapists are looking for.

Sometimes I meet a new client and everything they tell me (over the period of a few sessions) is someone else's fault. The reason they didn't finish their education. The reason they lose job after job. The reason they drink. The reason they yell far too much at their children. The reason relationships don't work. They take little ownership of their own destiny. They don't take accountability for what has transpired in their lives. This is glaring evidence that this person is not handling their life in a healthy way. They probably aren't making the best choices. They aren't processing information in a way that's productive. They live a life that breeds thoughts such as, *I can't control any of the bad things that happen to me, so why try?*

Not everything is someone else's fault. I have made mistakes. I can even look at my child's behavior and own some of theirs. Healthy people can evaluate what is under their control.

I'm embarrassed to say that I've backed into our garage door a couple of times. There are indentations that are proof of my mistakes. Both times, I've been distracted and stressed. I pressed that garage door button and backed up too quickly. I was typically running late or (gasp) looking at my phone. There's still a scratch on my Toyota that bears proof of these moments. The second time I did it, I called my husband to tell him the news. I was so angry. "We need a new garage door opener," I said. "This one's just too slow." I had convinced myself that I was not at fault and the speed of the device (which has remained the same since we have lived in this house for almost a decade) was at fault for the scratch and the dent. But I realized something important. I can't look at the scratch on my car or the dent in my garage and blame the machine. Yes, it's slow. Yes, it's old. But I am at fault for not managing the distractions. I can own that I am often to blame for running late. I backed into the garage. And taking ownership of the scratch and dent caused me to change my behavior that just may prevent me from doing it again.

## 3. THEY DON'T BLAME ONLY THEMSELVES FOR NEGATIVE CIRCUMSTANCES AND EXPERIENCES.

My friend sat in a doctor's office to get the news on her twelve-year-old's condition. Her doctor had the hard news to deliver that her child has a rare condition in the brain called Chiari malformation. This was causing her headaches. This condition isn't caused by external factors; it just happens. The good news is that it is treatable and can be cured by surgery. But neurosurgery, as well as any surgery, is scary.

Soon after getting this news, my friend surveyed her past. She thought about what she ate during pregnancy, how long she breastfed. The vaccines she signed for her daughter to receive. The fact is, she knew deep down that she was not to blame. Her daughter's brain had always been this way. But she blamed herself. And this was not healthy.

This is the opposite problem to the previous point. These people blame themselves for *everything*. The reason their mom has breast cancer is because they didn't push for them to have an earlier mammogram. The reason their marriage is struggling is because they gained fifteen pounds. The reason their baby cries too much is because they held her too much and "spoiled her." These women worry me because *when we take too much ownership of the hurt in our lives, then we discount the ownership that God has in our lives.*

## 4. THEY IDENTIFY AND RECOGNIZE THEIR TRIGGERS AND NEGATIVE EMOTIONS AND CREATE A PLAN TO HANDLE THEM.

In graduate school, they teach therapists that one of the most important things to do is to "know thyself." If we know ourselves well—thoroughly—we are going to know our own triggers and issues that can impact our ability to give solid, sound advice. We have to know ourselves in order to not project our own issues onto our clients. This helps us give ethical and godly advice to clients.

A few years ago, I noticed a big trigger for my anxiety. For some reason, I'm the world's most anxious hostess. For several years, we hosted a large community group for our church in my home. Every Sunday, I would wake up with a sense of dread. This was a great group of people who treated us very well. They loved us well. So, for me, my anxiety didn't make sense.

They didn't expect my home to be spotless. They didn't expect me to provide all of the snacks. However, I spent most of those Sundays anxious and distracted. I knew something had to change.

While we don't want to always avoid every trigger for our anxiety, sometimes we need to endure triggering situations in order to get through our fear. But during this season, we asked for another family to take over hosting duties.

It helped a lot. I was able to enjoy Sundays again. I didn't spend the entire church service making lists in my head for what I needed to get done. I was able to rest and be present with my babies. I made an attempt to know myself so that I could grow myself. I realized that I felt frustrated and overwhelmed with having two small children. I felt self-conscious about not being the best cook. I needed to know myself. These small moments of self-awareness set me up for growth and success.

I finally started to appreciate my triggers because they set up opportunities for growth and healing. Healthy people know that this is also a process that regularly needs to be reevaluated. We are growing and changing, and so will our triggers. The only way to know thyself is to incorporate self-care and to take time to do some deep self-exploration into your thoughts, issues, and behaviors.

*Know thyself to grow thyself.*

I'm still getting to know myself at middle age, and I have a feeling that there's still much more to learn. It's never too late to change. Believe me, my clients in their nineties have taught me this important truth. Today, right now, let's identify your triggers. Then reflect on what might be triggering you now.

## 5. THEY HAVE FOUND A WAY TO BE COMFORTABLE IN THEIR OWN SKIN.

Emotionally healthy moms have learned to like who they are, flaws and all. They have stopped apologizing for their imperfections. They have, in fact, embraced them. They have decided that they are amazing.

It was a Monday morning and I was talking to a client about dating. An adorable young professional, she had had several great conversations with a young man she met online. They were going to meet for the first time the following night. She talked to me about her apprehension about meeting face-to-face. She was nervous about whether he would find her attractive. She was nervous about finding him attractive. But most of all, she was anxious that he would find her "dorky." She was a clever and fun young woman, and I couldn't help but smile. She's charismatic, well-spoken, and charming. It never ceases to amaze me how inaccurate our perceptions of ourselves can be. She saw these qualities and considered herself dorky. So we worked with that.

A self-identified "dork" myself, I talked to her about being comfortable in her own skin. If she's silly and likes nerdy things, she should own it. Similar to what we talked about in chapter 5, sport it like a badge of honor. If we own it, no one can hijack it and make it their own. I'm fully confident in the fact that not everyone will like me. I am constantly spilling things and my ADHD is frustrating if it's not endearing. But I own my dorkiness. In doing so, I get to decide what it gets to do to me. No one else gets that power.

This self-identified dork wrote a book, makes friends, has a blast, has amazing children and a super-hot husband. So, own it. You can own that you have room for growth while believing you are beautiful and strong. If emotionally healthy people aren't there yet, they're actively working on it.

Decide that you're fun and great. If anyone is offended by your confidence, they're not real friends and these friendships aren't the ones that will lead to championship. You can have room for improvement while loving everything that God gave you. Make the decision to accept yourself, flaws and all.

6. THEY ACTIVELY FIGHT COMPARISON.

Even though we are probably all plagued with the thief named comparison, healthy people identify and fight against the propensity to compare themselves to others. They fight it faithfully.

I fully believe that we all struggle with comparing ourselves to others. I compare my kitchen cabinets to my friends' cabinets. I compare my body to the influencers' bodies. I compare my bank account to that of others. I will be compared as an author in terms of the sales of this book to the sales of other authors' works. It's sometimes necessary, sometimes damaging. The emotionally healthy mom knows the difference and fights against damaging comparison.

The healthy part of me can acknowledge that no matter how much I diet or exercise, I will never have the body that other women have. I stand 5 feet, 10 inches—I can't become short magically. I can't change my genetic code, which in its natural state "blessed me" with stretch marks. But I can accept the things I cannot change and learn to love and honor them.

## 7. THEY SURROUND THEMSELVES WITH PEOPLE WHO SUPPORT THEIR OWN PERSONAL HEALTH AND GROWTH.

Moms who are emotionally healthy limit interaction with truly toxic people. They attempt to seek healthy relationships with people who want to see them succeed. Of course, we all have had unhealthy relationships in our lives. However, healthy people set boundaries with toxic relationships and may even limit the amount of control and influence they let these people have in their lives. They seek close relationships with other people who support emotionally healthy lives—people who want to see you grow. Who seek the Lord. Who want good things for your life. Who don't celebrate when you fail. They respect the boundaries that you set.

I've seen this in my own life, especially in recent years. When I submitted my first proposal for this book, I had so many friends supporting me, encouraging me, and praying for me. They helped me workshop chapter titles, and they helped me edit and proofread. They shared my posts on social media and told me what was working and what was not. I had a team of solid supporters and helpers to get me through a very challenging two years of my life.

When I won Lysa TerKeurst's book contract, things seemed to change. I started to feel a few of these voices fade. It seemed several friends were no longer rooting for me to succeed. And then one friend overtly told me that she was not supportive of this life-changing opportunity. "Rachael, this book will never sell. No one wants to read a book about struggling as a new mom. You don't have many followers, you're not famous, and I just think this whole thing is ridiculous," she said.

At first, I was in shock. I hadn't asked her for advice. This comment came out of the blue. We were simply catching up while watching our kids play in her backyard. I asked some follow-up questions and she wanted to change the subject. At the time, she had never read a single word I had written. She didn't have much, if any, information on which to base this claim. She wasn't trying to help me; she was rooting for me to fail.

When I say I cried myself to sleep that night, I mean I cried for a week. I lost my appetite. No amount of makeup could cover the impact that these words had on my heart. This is a person who mattered to me, and she still does. And I felt, and still feel, that God called me to write the words you, my dear sister, are reading at this very moment.

A week later, my counselor talked through this relationship with me. This friend had a history of codependent and toxic behavior. The history of our relationship had become clear, even though this was extremely painful. Her words were the opposite of kind. And sadly, this dynamic had gone on for over a decade.

After a lot of talking, thinking, and prayer, I decided to distance myself from this friendship. As hard as losing a friend can be, my choice to set giant boundaries was a sign of my emotional health. I was able to value myself enough to expect that a friend would build me up, not tear me down.

From this moment on, I started realizing that I needed to value God more than a friendship. I needed to identify when another person was intentionally and repeatedly causing harm so I could have the courage to risk friend loss in the hopes of investing in a healthier friendship. The good news is that God, as he usually does, provided an amazing friendship to take its place.

## 8. THEY ARE ADAPTABLE AND RESILIENT.

Although it's hard, emotionally healthy people are somehow able to laugh at the unpredictability of life. A rock hits their windshield, the stove breaks, a miscommunication happens, spit-up ends up on their shirt—and they can eventually laugh at how ridiculous life and motherhood can often be. They accept that this is part of the human experience. They 100 percent believe that they can do hard things.

I remember a moment I knew I was getting better. I was back at work from maternity leave. It was a stressful time. But I was sleeping, on meds, and in therapy. I was washing my hair. I was making sure I was taking care of myself and of my relationships. I was getting emotionally healthy as a new mom.

On this drive to work, I was late. I had a new client. I needed to not mess this up. I needed to get paid in order to take care of all of the bills we couldn't pay while I was out on leave. Suddenly, a huge rock came out of nowhere on the highway and split my windshield into a set of spiderweb-shaped cracks right in front of my eyes.

Disheveled and shaken up, I safely pulled my car off to the side of the highway, thankful I wasn't hurt. Now, this event a month prior would have done more than left me irritated and upset. A month prior to me becoming emotionally healthy, it would have ruined my day. I would have called my mom and/or husband in tears. I would have been so upset over not wanting to pay for a new windshield.

I remember this moment clearly—my exact thought was, *Worst-case scenario, I have to buy a new windshield if insurance won't cover it and I'll put $200 on my credit card. Oh well. Life happens.*

I think I even laughed a few minutes later. I was resilient and adaptable, and I wasn't deciding that the day was ruined. I didn't assume that the worst was going to happen. I approached an unfortunate everyday problem with a realistic and hopeful stance that God calls us to have.

## 9. THEY RENOUNCE PERFECTIONISM.

They actively fight against the desire to have the perfect body, home, number of Instagram followers, etc. Not that they don't try to "live their best life," but living the best life doesn't mean perfection. They face life with a sense of resiliency to the ebbs and flows of this world.

I have a friend who has struggled over the years with an eating disorder. She has sought treatment and was able to overcome this painful and destructive mental illness. I watched her recover as we were in our twenties. I remember seeing her carefully inspect her body in the mirror, scanning for any possible flaw.

Then she got pregnant. I remember thinking, *Uh oh. What is this going to be like?* I had already had a baby at this point—I knew what she was up against. How would she cope? Would she relapse?

Fast-forward to her having a toddler and her beautiful moment of emotional health. She unwrapped powdered lemon-flavored donuts and handed them out to our children. Then she did something that shocked me: she ate one too.

She never—and I mean never—would have done this years ago. And if she had a teensy bite of something decadent, she would later punish herself in the gym for hours. She looked at me with a smile and said, "Rachael, sometimes I eat a donut and sometimes I don't. Either way, it's okay."

I waited for the quintessential *but* to come into this conversation. But it never occurred. She didn't justify her choice to eat something delicious. Now I know that eating a donut isn't the definition of a flaw. But to this dear friend, she was accepting her humanity and rejecting the idea that perfection is achievable or even desirable, especially at the expense of her child.

*

One of the biggest mistakes a new mom can make during this part of her journey is when she starts to forget or discount how far she's already come. I mean, talk about demotivational, right? But I see it almost every day. A woman comes to see me for two months and she's worked her tail off. Then she ignores giant steps she's taken or decides that those giant steps were teensy. She doesn't give herself credit for the hard work she has already put into herself. She ignores the boundaries she's set, the postpartum plan, the victories, the self-care, the changes in her thinking, the healing.

There may be nothing that the Enemy would love more than for you to ignore all of the good that God has just done in your life. I know this next exercise may seem like a lot, but let's be determined not to ignore your progress. Let's put your pen to paper and actually draw how far you've come. This image is powerful and I pray it will help you keep going, even when the days are hard and messy. Once it's done, you can't ignore that these goals have, in fact, been accomplished.

And mama, these are giant steps, *never* tiny, okay?

# Postpartum Progress Bottle

- ← Can say out loud that "I'm a good mom"
- ← Studied God's scorecard for motherhood
- ← Sought God to know that "I'm being anointed, not afflicted"
- ← Scheduled something to look forward to
- ← Gave myself permission to grieve what I've lost
- ← Tried three new ways to bond with my baby
- ← Wrote my thank-you letter to my body
- ← Told an ugly thought to go away
- ← Identified intrusive thoughts
- ← Listed childhood wounds and named a cornerstone wound
- ← Identified anxiety and anger triggers
- ← Identified what it means to be a good mom
- ← Accepted that it's okay to not love motherhood
- ← Spoke out about my struggles on a safe online forum
- ← Refused to stay shameful of my emotional struggles
- ← Asked for someone to bring me snacks
- ← Filled out my Postpartum Wellness Plan
- ← Decided if I should see a counselor
- ← Made time for one self-care action each day
- ← Asked for people to check on me
- ← Commissioned my Postpartum Pack
- ← Shared with three people that I'm struggling
- ← Opened this book
- ← Prayed for myself and my baby today

**Directions: Color from the bottom to the top as you've worked on each of these major milestones.** This way you'll be able to visually keep track of your progress by filling in your postpartum baby bottle, which is similar to filling up a thermometer to meet a goal. This practical method will help you when your heart wants to discount your victories.

Track your progress, mama. And once you've recognized every milestone on your journey, take some time to celebrate it!

# Conclusion

## *Rivers in the Wasteland*

I didn't know it was possible, but I have two favorite verses in the Bible. Years ago, a handful of my clients quoted the same verse to me, out of the blue. (Side note: the irony of being a Christian counselor is that many times my clients teach me just as much as I teach them.) I felt chills running down my spine. I knew that God was speaking to me.

> Forget the former things;
>> do not dwell on the past.
>
> See, I am doing a new thing!
>> Now it springs up; do you not perceive it?
>
> I am making a way in the wilderness
>> and streams in the wasteland.
>
> (ISAIAH 43:18–19)

My heart, my weary heart, felt like the wasteland. Old, lifeless, with nothing left to give. No thirst to quench. It was a land where nothing could grow. No fruit to bear. I gave and gave to my infant son. And deep in the trenches of PPD, I felt lifeless, a drought cracking my lips.

There's a chalkboard sign in my office. In my messy lettering, I wrote in chalk "Rivers in the Wasteland." I erased the words several times. I used different chalk. The words were messy. I kept writing it again and again because my chalkboard is never quite Pinterest-worthy. But it was beautiful. Smeared chalk and all, I left the sign to hang. The messy sign and the smeared letters were a symbol of what I am. My messy letters remind me of the truth and hope that we have in Jesus. By his promise to make *all things new*, we are reminded of his promise of Philippians 1:6: "He who began a good work in you will carry it on to completion until the day of Christ Jesus."

Not only does he promise to make all things new, but his Word promises that our story will have an ending—not a sad one with tears of pain, but an ending that promises new beginnings. This ending is when *a mom is born.*

An ending when you are made into something new—a mother. An ending where you start your baby's beginnings. God is bringing it to completion in you. I believe these verses are the truth of what God is doing in you right this very moment.


## FORGET THE FORMER THINGS; DO NOT DWELL ON THE PAST

For all intents and purposes, I felt I had failed the first three months of motherhood. I had moments where I was afraid to be alone with my son. There were days I struggled to do everything it took to take care of him. It's still hard to admit that I needed as much help as I did. There were moms who didn't seem to need the help that I needed during that season. But that wasn't me. And that's okay. I had to put him in his crib and let him cry while I cried in the next room. I had to ask for help more times than I could count.

But God. He had something to say to me on this day. I believe he has something to say to you today.

Forgive yourself for the ways that you feel like you failed. I felt like I had failed at soothing my baby. So often he just cried until eventually something that I had done, whether intentionally or unintentionally, worked. Or until he tired himself out. These were truly desperate days. I don't know why, in my cloud of PPD, I felt like I was defective as a mother. Like an iPhone that was missing an essential piece of hardware. Something on that impressive assembly line did not get installed. But God calls us to forget the former things. I believe in this moment he is calling you to move forward. I want you to take a moment to say out loud, "I forgive myself. I am a good mom."

What does it look like to forget the former things? Maybe you need to own that God never promises us that motherhood will be easy. It means that you need to grieve that your life will never be the same. It means that it is time to embrace your new identity as mother, wife, worker, sister, daughter, and friend. Now is the time to come to terms with the fact that trips to Target will not look the same for quite some time. It means that you are accepting the grace that God has for you.

You know what else happens when you forget the former things? Something beautiful. Something groundbreaking. Life will never be the same—it will be better.

Your life will be full of moments cuddling with your children before bedtime and watching them grow. Your life will be filled with their first smiles, giggles, and kisses. You will get to watch their eyes light up the first time they decorate a Christmas tree. You will laugh at the pure joy on their faces the first time they taste an Oreo. I pray that you will see your child become a believer. Your life will be full in the way that God intended when he created you.

# SEE, I AM DOING A NEW THING

The endless rocking, the expensive glider that wasn't the perfect gliding motion for my baby, the squats, the swaddling attempts, the special leg stretches to relieve gas for my baby, the pediatrician's appointments—the countless efforts weren't wasted. Those efforts grew me into the mom that I am today. They were all a part of God's plan of refining me through the metamorphosis of motherhood. Most importantly, my tears weren't wasted. They are no longer a wasteland. God was doing a *new* thing in me. God was doing a *new* thing in my son. God wants to do a *new* thing in you at this very moment.

A couple of years ago I got an email from my son's teacher. He was only in the first grade. She wanted to speak to me. That couldn't be good. "What has he done this time?" I said to myself while rolling my eyes. My son is a great student, but like most boys his age, he struggles to focus and sit still. I walked into the teacher's room with my head hung low like so many parents do when we think our children are in trouble. My heart was racing. My anxiety started to spin like a hamster wheel.

My son's teacher started to explain. There was a boy in my son's class who is developmentally delayed. This student was struggling with angry outbursts and fits of crying. This child didn't have many friends. He was teased a lot. Most days, no one would join him for lunch or play with him at recess.

I started to think, *No. Please Lord, not this. Anything but this.* I felt the awful shame of how I had royally screwed up as a mother. I yelled at him that time when he was squalling in his crib. This is my fault. He's broken because of me. I didn't hold him enough. No—I did it too much. Maybe I should have let him "cry it out." I was too depressed to care for my son. I did this. And my PPD made it a hundred times worse.

The teacher continued:

Hunt has started helping him with his schoolwork. He defended him on the playground while another child was teasing him. He's started having lunch with this child. He offers hugs when he starts to cry. He talks to him when he has angry outbursts. It's almost like he's *adopted* him because he wants to help. But now Hunt is being teased for standing up for him.

My life was full up to this point. And a childless life can absolutely be full. But you, dear sister, have been called to motherhood. Hearing this teacher tell me about my son's action brought me feelings of joy and fulfillment that won't fade. It will not cease. I felt pride, but pride in the okay way. It was the feeling that I had done something right with this extraordinary baby. He was doing *good* in the world. He was starting to impact people around him. He was doing good when I wasn't looking. He was standing up for justice when it wasn't popular. He was putting himself and his own selfishness on the altar for someone who was under attack.

Then it hit me. If my seven-year-old can put his own desires, his perceived popularity, his selfishness on the altar, I certainly can too. I can forget the former things. I can forget what it was like to have a tummy without stretch marks. I can be okay not having a home with smooth walls without scuff marks. I can put my travel plans on hold. All because I'm building a legacy. Travel won't do that. A pristine home won't do that. A flat tummy won't do that. But having these children and watching them grow will. And putting ourselves and our plans on the altar is what God is asking us to do as mothers.

There's nothing greater in my life than these moments. I have a legacy. Not a legacy of a lot of money. There's no giant family diamond. No legacy of being particularly extraordinary or famous. It's unlikely that I will be written about in a newspaper article when I pass away someday. But I do have the legacy that my babies, my children, will be the hands and feet of Jesus long after I'm unable to. This can be true for you too, as long as you are willing. You will have a *legacy*. You will be loved with a love that is unlike any other earthly love.

## NOW IT SPRINGS UP: DO YOU NOT PERCEIVE IT?

God made a plan. I made a plan. I swallowed my pride with the pill. I assembled my Postpartum Pack. I spoke. I asked for help. I refused to wear the shroud of shame from sadness and anxiety. I refused to keep silent about my struggle. I brought the truth to the surface as a geyser springs forth. I couldn't have stopped it even if I had wanted to. God was doing a mighty work in me.

My husband and I regularly take my boys on "wilderness adventures." We strap on our boots and pick a park to explore. My boys love hiking and exploring nature. They kick over the leaves, find beaten-down paths, and climb to find the best view. They especially love a good creek where they can search for crawdads, fish, and other wildlife. The true prize for my boys is when they get to see an animal in its natural habitat.

One recent wilderness adventure was truly special. We had just finished a 5k hike with both of my boys. Their little legs were tired, as were mine. We came to a steep drop-off with a ravine. We carefully approached to see a creek. To my surprise, we hadn't scared off what we were about to see. At the bottom of the ravine was a beaver dam. And right beside it was a beaver building her home. It was hard to see her if you didn't squint. It was hard to see her if I didn't know to look. I had to know what a beaver dam looked like to notice her. Lo and behold, she was working hard at shoring up her dwelling for winter.

I shushed my boys and said, "Look." They tiptoed up to the edge of the ravine to see what I was trying to show them. I didn't want them to miss it. I said again, "Look down right there," as I pointed a finger in the desired viewing direction. My older son whispered (quite loudly), "Mom, a beaver!" My younger son said, "Where?!" I did what mothers do over and over again. I repeated myself so that they would get the point. I wanted them to get it. I wanted them to listen. I said it again so that they would have a chance to learn. I quieted my rather loud offspring a second time to get them to see what I was trying to show them. "Look—right there, Reeve."

When God repeats himself in Scripture, he's trying to get our attention. It's always for a purpose. *He doesn't want us to miss it.* Like that day with my boys in the woods, he doesn't want us to miss the blessing right before our eyes. "Shhhh," I imagine God saying to me so many times. He wants us to get quiet and pause so that we can squint to see. *Don't you perceive it?*

Don't miss it, friend. Don't miss out on opening your eyes to the progress you've made. How have you dodged the traps in your trek? How have you learned to stay calm with your child, even sometimes? List the moments that you have started to *delight* in your baby. How have you managed your triggers? I believe every verse in Scripture is God-breathed. Ordained. Every line and every verse is written for you and me. Since it is ordained, then this phrase is here for a reason. It is God-breathed for you and me to read it. God is making sure we get the point. *Do you not perceive it?* Say it. Own it. Shout it from the rooftops.

"I learned to be a mom and I learned to be the kind of mom that this baby, this exact tiny human needed!"

## I AM MAKING A WAY IN THE WILDERNESS AND STREAMS IN THE WASTELAND

In the last few years, I have prayed for God to give me a "word" for the year ahead. In 2018, I never felt like I was given a word. I prayed and prayed, and for some reason or another, he chose not to give me one. In 2019, God gave me a clear word: *heal.* As I was given a word to pray about for that calendar year, I was so excited about the relationships and emotional wounds I was going to get to heal from. Little did I know that I would soon break my tailbone (shatter, rather) and spend the year in pain. Also, I would have complications from an unrelated surgery that would require two unexpected, subsequent surgeries. So *heal* being my word became a joke in my circle of friends. *Seriously God, I'm not loving this,* I thought as I found where I had written my 2019 word in big letters at the top of a notebook. I never thought that he meant it to be so literal. But that's what I did that year. I learned about myself. I made a lot of decisions about taking better care of my physical health. And I healed—a lot.

As 2019 came to an end, I didn't pray for a word for the new decade year. I didn't need another 2019. (Oh, how I'm snickering at writing this paragraph.) I thought, *2019 was so bad, 2020 has to be better.* Of course, we now know that 2020 is a year that will no doubt go down in history for many reasons. All I was thinking about in 2019 was nursing my physical body back to health. I never considered what was ahead. Social injustices, political unrest, a chaotic election, and of course, the global pandemic.

I didn't have to pray for a word for 2020. God gave me one without asking. I cringed when I heard it and it jumped out and grabbed me by my earlobes. "New," he said. My mind began to race. What horrible omen could this be? *New*? New *job*? New *house,* maybe? I thought, *I can't fathom moving right now. I love my job. I don't want anything new outside of the clothing and home furnishings arena.*

The year 2020 became the year that I would learn to teach my boys virtually. It was the year that we lived more simply and things slowed down. It was the year that God called me to start writing the very book that you're reading.

I never thought I had what it took to be a good mom. But here I am. *My tears made a puddle on my baby's head. Then they led to rivers in the wasteland.* They led to my learning to help other women. Where once all hope was lost, it was now found. The thirst was quenched. He makes all things new.

Once you were in one of the darkest and most hopeless moments of your life. Against all odds, you have shot down the Enemy's lies. You have learned to be a mom. You have found new ways to take care of yourself. You have identified and fought intrusive thoughts. Maybe you talked to your doctor about swallowing your pride with swallowing a pill. You've sought wise and godly counsel. You've read a book in the middle of your crazy schedule. Your pain has led to rivers in the wasteland. You have learned that you have what it takes to be a good mom.

Look at all you've accomplished. Do a little dance. Jump up and down. I certainly am.

Now go forth—find purpose in your pain. Join a new mom's Postpartum Pack. Bring her snacks. Hold her baby while she puts her mascara on. Do some squats with that baby. When you're triggered, look at this list. Remember the truth that you have won. Pray for your baby. Repeat. And celebrate motherhood as it was created to be.

# Appendix

## *How Do You Know If You Need Therapy?*

Y ou may be thinking you don't need to talk to a therapist. That's cool. We can still be friends. You may think only crazy people go to therapy. The truth is, the sanest, coolest, and most levelheaded people I've ever met have sat on the couch across from me as clients. They know that we sometimes need someone else's perspective in order to understand our own.

This therapist has seen a therapist on and off since I was twenty years old. I've always said every truly great therapist has had a therapist. We are not immune from the issues that plague others. In fact, we typically are riddled with the same issues, or even worse. It's part of what draws us to this field of work. For me to be a good wife, a good mom, and a good therapist, I go to therapy. And perhaps you should consider doing the same.

Therapy isn't what you might think it is. It's a powerful thing to sit across from a stranger who has no investment in lying to you or telling you what you want to hear. It's a strength like no other to then hear them validate what you're going through.

Not everyone needs therapy. However, everyone can benefit from therapy.

The really amazing thing about therapy is how God speaks to me through that fifty-minute time slot. How the Holy Spirit stirs in me in a way to help others heal—to assist in navigating the struggle. He helps me say, *Yes, being a mom is really hard.*

So how do you know if you need therapy? Here are ten behaviors that might direct you in making that decision:

1. **You are having trouble making decisions.** Are you finding yourself overwhelmed with decisions that you used to make without blinking? Does even making simple decisions seem difficult?

2. **You have a negative thought or set of thoughts that don't stop.** You find yourself having thoughts that circle around and won't go away no matter what you do or who you talk to.

3. **Things you usually enjoy have lost their fun and excitement.** The birthday party that you always look forward to doesn't seem alluring. You aren't excited about planning a vacation this year even though you loved doing this in the past. That Christmas gift that you asked for and received just doesn't make you smile.

4. **You are crying more than usual and/or having angry outbursts.** Have you cried twice this week and it's out of the norm? Have you yelled at your kids throughout the day when it's not warranted?

5. **You're avoiding social situations.** Have you started avoiding church when you used to look forward to going every week? Have you canceled social plans for no reason other than not wanting to go? Do you avoid people at work who you would normally enjoy talking to?

6. **You are having trouble sleeping at night.** Your worries

keep you up at night. You find yourself having several restless nights back-to-back.

7. **You use unhealthy ways to cope.** You may overeat or use substances to deal with stress, anxiety, or sadness. If you find yourself saying or thinking, "I need a drink," please call a counselor or pastor.

8. **You're experiencing feelings of hopelessness.** You might even find yourself feeling like there's nothing to look forward to.

9. **Your relationships are struggling and/or strained.** This might seem like a given, especially after having a new baby. But if you find yourself in stressed relationships with a friend or family member, you might need to talk with someone who is outside of your social circle.

10. **You have experienced a major loss.** A job, a relationship, a death, a home—it all comes down to loss. You may need to spend some time grieving this loss with a trained therapist.

Don't do this alone. We are meant to have different people disciple us throughout our lives. Let us help you. If you've determined you need to see someone, here are some things to consider.

1. Choose someone licensed, even if they are provisionally licensed in the state that they work in.

   Someone licensed has gone through the necessary avenues to achieve a really hard thing. They have counseled people for thousands of hours before even sitting in front of you. They are held accountable to a set of laws and ethical standards. They have proven that they know enough about this field to, at the very least, do no harm. They have the skills to do good and to aid in the healing process.

2. Consider seeing a Christian counselor.

There are so many incredible therapists out there. I have seen several therapists in my career. Unfortunately, I have struggled to connect with someone who does not understand the importance of my faith. We don't make decisions just on what makes us happy or what makes us feel good. If I subscribed to some of the feel-good psychology out there, I would have made a lot of ungodly mistakes. A lot of hearts would have been wounded. I'm not sure I would still be married. And I definitely wouldn't be a good counselor.

In my counseling practice, I use the exact same tools and techniques that any secular therapist would use. I have the same training as a secular therapist. In many ways, it's really not that different.

However, there's one major difference: secular therapy bases its treatment on theory. Many Christian counselors use theory and truth—the truth of what God says about us and our actions. Now, theory matters a lot. However, for many Christian counselors, truth and the Word of God matter more than theory. Truth trumps theory.

Of course, there's nothing wrong with seeing a secular therapist. But if you are a Christian, I would suggest first looking for a therapist who understands the role of faith in your life, your health, and your decisions.

As a therapist, I don't tell people to do what feels good. I tell people to do what is right. If you do what is right, then God will honor that and he will be glorified.

3. Trust is the foundation of quality therapy.

Trust is the foundation of every relationship—with your accountant, with your friends, with your coworkers. And definitely with your therapist. I always say it like this: Does it feel like this person helping you really cares about you? If the answer is no, it sounds like it's not the right fit. Thank you, but next . . .

# HOW DO YOU KNOW YOU'RE
# IN THE RIGHT PLACE?

It's been studied a lot. In the psychology world we call it "client engagement," or the strength of the therapeutic relationship. We know one thing to be true: It's not the counselor having the same race, gender, or personal style as their client. It's not whether they are a master's level clinician or a doctorate level. After a therapist has a handful of years under their belt, the bond between client and therapist has little to do with years of experience. It has to do completely with how much you connect with and trust the professional sitting across from you. You should feel like your therapist cares about you. If not, please explore other options for getting your mental health needs met.

# Acknowledgments

How do I say thank-you to people who haven't just changed my life but possibly changed the lives of thousands of women? Without them this book wouldn't have made it into many moms' hands. The impact here is beyond measure.

To Mitch: You're the best man I've ever known. You held me up through my postpartum depression, and you've held me up through this project. You're as much an author of this book as I am. I love you more every day I get to be with you.

To my boys, Hunt and Reeve: You have both been so patient with me while I wrote this book. For the many times I had to work late on edits and even the times I couldn't be there for you, thank you. You had so much grace for me when my answer was regularly, "Not now, sweetie." You both are the best thing that's ever happened to me. Every day I can't believe I get to be a mom to you both. I love you, Hunt and Reeve. I can't wait to watch you learn and grow through each of the days ahead of us.

To my mom: I'm so thankful that I get to be your daughter. Every day with you is a gift. You taught me about Jesus, you gave me a home, and you continue to be a rock-solid source of unwavering support. Thank you for never giving up on me.

To my family by marriage, particularly Karen and Joe Elmore:

Thank you for everything you did to make sure my career happened. Thank you for loving on my boys while I worked long days. You continue to be the most amazing and loving family to me. I'm proud that you're my people.

To Meredith Brock: My agent, my confidant, my prayer partner, my beloved Enneagram 8 who challenged me, believed in me, and fought for me. Your faith and talent fostered in me exactly what I needed as a new author.

To Lysa TerKeurst and the team at Proverbs 31 Ministries: You listened to the struggles of new moms. You didn't look away. You recognized that new moms struggle hard, and you laid the foundation for me to offer help to as many women as need it. Time and time again your team encouraged me, prayed for me, and inspired me. Thank you for playing a vital part in getting this message into the hands that need it most.

To my writing coach, Nicki Koziarz: You were the first person to believe in me and in my message. You made me the writer that I am today. You never took the easy way out—you challenged me to be better with every sentence I wrote.

To my Bible study—Ryan, Emily, Lori, Kelli, Clara, Virginia, Lynda, Jessica, Taryn, Stephanie, and Dalissia: You all prayed for me, watched my children, fed me, listened to me, read early chapters, helped me brainstorm titles, encouraged me, and didn't let me give up. Most important, you pointed me to my faith first over any obstacle I was facing. I love each of you to my core.

To Abby: You never let me give up. And I tried. I can't recall a day in the past three years when we haven't spoken at least once about my book. About how you could help me. About what ideas were good and which ones were bad. You've been my friend, editor, and unofficial therapist throughout this journey.

To my dear friends—Alexas, Rici, the Bohannon family, Mary Gray, Vicky, Samantha, Lee, and Ann: You all got me through my postpartum depression. You brought me tacos and listened to me cry. You loved me when it was ugly. You helped me heal from the inside out. Thank you for your unwavering support and deep friendship. I love you all.

To the amazing community of moms of Mountain Island—Sabrina, Jen, Kelley, Lindsay, Melody, Courtney, Kristen, Jenny, Roxanne, Vicki, Lisa, and Heather: You each unknowingly taught me to be a mom. Thank you for going before me, listening to me, giving me solid advice, and making me laugh through motherhood.

To my author friends—Meredith, Nicole, Lauren, Taylor, Christy, Julie, and my COMPEL writing cohort group: You all have been my authorship "spirit guides." During the many late-night calls, texts, and panicked moments when I needed you to fix whatever I needed done, you all did it. You always helped when I would say, "How in the world do I ___?" Thank you.

The entire team that made this book possible—Kathryn, Brigitta, and the rest of the team at Thomas Nelson: You spent countless hours helping me refine this book to be what it is today. Thank you for not just saying, "It looks good." You didn't take the easy way out. I'm glad you gave me hard, honest feedback that made this book truly great.

To my clients: There are tens of thousands of you out there. You have entrusted me with your mental health, your marriages, your children. You have believed in me enough to help me learn to be a better therapist every year of my career. I see each of your faces in my dreams. Your words live in the halls of my house. I've never forgotten you, even though there have been so many. You have each taught me the lessons I needed to write a book to help so many people. From the bottom of my heart, thank you.

# Notes

## Introduction

1. "What Is Postpartum Depression and Anxiety?," American Psychological Association, 2008, https://www.apa.org/pi/women/resources/reports/postpartum-depression.
2. "Baby Blues After Pregnancy," March of Dimes, last updated May 2021, https://www.marchofdimes.org/pregnancy/baby-blues-after-pregnancy.aspx#.

## Chapter 1: The Tears on My Baby Are Mine

1. *Diagnostic and Statistical Manual of Mental Disorders*: *DSM-IV*, (Washington, DC: American Psychiatric Association, 2000), 422.
2. "Postpartum Depression," Mayo Clinic, last updated November 24, 2022, https://www.mayoclinic.org/diseases-conditions/postpartum-depression/symptoms-causes/syc-20376617.
3. Christin Perry, "What to Expect with Postpartum Hormone Changes," *Parents*, updated August 7, 2022, https://www.parents.com/pregnancy/my-body/postpartum/postpartum-hormone-changes/.

## Chapter 2: Hold My Baby and Bring Me Snacks

1. Joseph T. Hallinan, "The Remarkable Power of Hope," *Psychology Today*, May 7, 2014, https://www.psychologytoday.com/us/blog/kidding-ourselves/201405/the-remarkable-power-hope.

## Chapter 3: A Mom with a Plan

1. Saul McLeod, "Maslow's Hierarchy of Needs," Simply Psychology, updated April 4, 2022, https://www.simplypsychology.org/maslow.html.
2. "What Kinds of Safety Checks Do Planes Undergo Before They Fly?," *Forbes*, October 18, 2017, https://www.forbes.com/sites/quora/2017/10/18/what-kinds-of-safety-checks-do-planes-undergo-before-they-fly/.

## Chapter 4: Dad Up

1. Deuteronomy 10:18; Psalm 82:3; Isaiah 1:17; John 14:18; James 1:27, 2:15–16.
2. Paul Hemez and Chanell Washington, "Number of Children Living Only with Their Mothers Has Doubled in Past 50 Years," United States Census Bureau, April 12, 2021, https://www.census.gov/library/stories/2021/04/number-of-children-living-only-with-their-mothers-has-doubled-in-past-50-years.html.

## Chapter 5: You Are Not a Bad Mom

1. Nancy Gapasin Gnass, "The Perfect Parent," Parenting with Teacher Nancy, May 19, 2017, https://www.parentingwithteachernancy.org/2017/05/the-perfect-parent.html.

## Chapter 7: The Four Horsemen of the Momocalypse

1. *Merriam-Webster.com Dictionary*, s.v. "shame," accessed September 15, 2022, https://www.merriam-webster.com/dictionary/shame.
2. Jim Folk, "Anxiety Disorder Statistics and Facts," AnxietyCentre.com, November 20, 2021, https://www.anxietycentre.com/statistics/anxiety-disorder-statistics-facts/.
3. "Anxiety Disorders," NAMI, updated December 2017, https://www.nami.org/About-Mental-Illness/Mental-Health-Conditions/Anxiety-Disorders.
4. "Endorphins: The Brain's Natural Pain Reliever," Harvard Health Publishing, July 20, 2021, https://www.health.harvard.edu/mind-and-mood/endorphins-the-brains-natural-pain-reliever.

## Chapter 8: Ugly Thoughts Living Rent-Free

1. Randy Dotinga, "Most People Have Unwanted Thoughts, International Study Finds," WebMD, May 9, 2014, https://www .webmd.com/mental-health/news/20140509/most-people-have -unwanted-thoughts-international-study-finds.

2. Prakhar Verma, "Destroy Negativity from Your Mind with This Simple Exercise," Medium, November 27, 2017, https://medium .com/the-mission/a-practical-hack-to-combat-negative-thoughts-in -2-minutes-or-less-cc3d1bddb3af.

3. Michele Molitor, "The Power of Your Brain | The 95–5% Rule," LinkedIn, October 5, 2019, https://www.linkedin.com/pulse/95–5 -rule-michele-molitor-cpcc-pcc-rtt-c-hyp?trk=portfolio_article-card _title.

4. *Merriam-Webster.com Dictionary*, s.v. "lovely," accessed September 15, 2022, https://www.merriam-webster.com/dictionary /lovely.

## Chapter 10: Put on the Mascara

1. *Merriam-Webster.com Legal Dictionary*, s.v. "net worth," accessed December 8, 2022, https://www.merriam-webster.com/legal/net %20worth.

2. Lisa Fields, "6 Ways Pets Can Improve Your Health," WebMD, October 24, 2013, https://www.webmd.com/hypertension-high -blood-pressure/features/6-ways-pets-improve-your-health.

## Chapter 11: Swallowing My Pride by Swallowing a Pill

1. Siang Yong Tan and Jason Merchant, "Frederick Banting (1891– 1941): Discoverer of Insulin," *Singapore Medical Journal* 58, no. 1 (January 2017): 2–3, https://www.ncbi.nlm.nih.gov/pmc/article /PMC5331123/.

## Chapter 12: A Soft Place to Cling

1. Robin Karr-Morse and Meredith S. Wiley, *Ghosts from the Nursery*, (New York: Grove Atlantic, 2007), 185.

2. Carissa Stephens, "How to Soothe Your Baby's Tummy Troubles,"

Healthline, September 16, 2021, https://www.healthline.com
/health/baby/baby-upset-stomach.

3. Saul McLeod, "Harry Harlow, Monkey Love Experiments," Simply
Psychology, 2020, https://www.simplypsychology.org/harlow
-monkey.html.

4. "Harlow's Classic Studies Revealed the Importance of Maternal
Contact," Association for Psychological Science, June 20, 2018,
https://www.psychologicalscience.org/publications/observer
/obsonline/harlows-classic-studies-revealed-the-importance-of
-maternal-contact.html.

5. Rebecca Buffum Taylor, "Your Baby's First Words," WebMD,
October 3, 2022, https://www.webmd.com/parenting/baby-talk
-your-babys-first-words.

6. Karr-Morse and Wiley, *Ghosts from the Nursery,* 185.

## Chapter 13: To Have and to Hold

1. Benjamin Hardy, "How to Learn a New Skill Well Enough to Do
It Automatically," *Fast Company*, April 5, 2016, https://www
.fastcompany.com/3058572/how-to-learn-a-new-skill-well-enough
-to-do-it-automaticall.

2. "Patience Definition," Google's English Dictionary, accessed
October 20, 2022, https://www.google.com/search?q=patience
+definition.

## Chapter 14: A Mom Who Doesn't Quit

1. Melissa Basgall, "Something to Do, Someone to Love, Something
to Look Forward To," Macaroni KID Kansas City, October 18,
2019, https://kansascityks.macaronikid.com/articles
/5da9d2fc1d49af6471d8c5c4/something-to-do%2C-someone-to
-love%2C-something-to-look-forward-to.